RICHMOND *Handbooks*

Series Editor : Paul Seligson

The
Mixed
Ability
Class

Julie Tice

Richmond
PUBLISHING

Richmond Publishing
19 Berghem Mews
Blythe Road
London W14 0HN

© Julie Tice 1997
Published by Richmond Publishing ®
First published 1997

ISBN: 84-294-4927-2
Depòsito legal: M-22032-2000
Printed in Spain by Palgraphic, S.A.

Design   Jonathan Barnard
Layout   Gecko Limited
Cover Design Geoff Sida, Ship Design

Illustrations   Steve Lach, Gecko Ltd, John Plumb & Liz Roberts

Publisher's Acknowledgement
The poem on page 62 (*The Duck*) is reprinted by permission of Curtis Brown, Ltd.
Copyright © 1940 by Ogden Nash, renewed.

Photographs   Colorific, page 35.

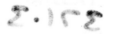

Map of the book

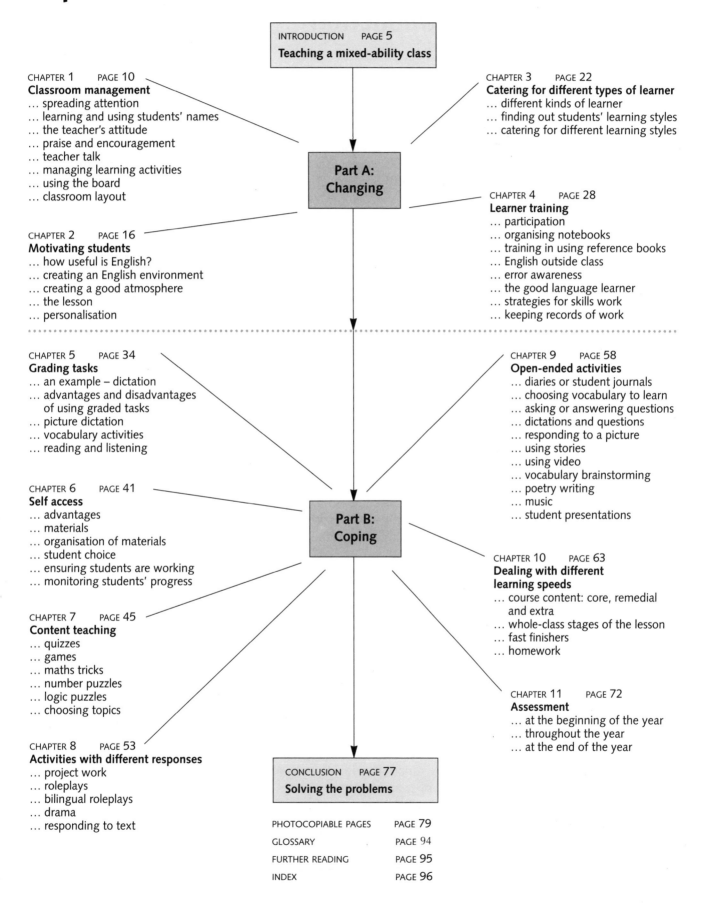

Richmond Handbooks for Teachers: An introduction

This series presents key issues in English Language Teaching today, to help you keep in touch with topics raised in recent educational reforms. The books all contain a mixture of analysis, development work, ideas and photocopiable resources for the classroom. The key note throughout is what is **practical**, **realistic** and **easy to implement**. Our aim is to provide a useful resource which will help you to develop your own teaching and to enjoy it more.

While each of the books has been written for the practising English Language Teacher in the primary or secondary environment, they are also suitable for teachers of languages other than English, as well as for teachers of young adults, trainee teachers and trainers.

All classroom activities are designed for lower-level classes (from beginners to lower intermediate) as these form the majority of classes in both primary and secondary. Most of them can, however, be easily adapted to higher levels.

The books all contain:

- *a section of photocopiable activities and templates.* These are either for immediate classroom use (some with a little adaptation to suit your classes) or for use throughout the year, e.g. assessment record sheets or project work planners.

- *regular development tasks.* These ask you to reflect on your teaching in the light of what you have just read, and some ask you to try new ideas in the class. They are all intended to make the ideas in the books more accessible to you as a classroom teacher.

- *an index of activities.* As most teachers dip into or skim through resource books, there is an index at the back of each book to help you find the sections or ideas that you wish to read about.

- *a comprehensive glossary.* As one of the main principles of the books is ease of use, the authors have tried not to use jargon or difficult terminology. Where this has been unavoidable, the word/term is in SMALL CAPITALS and is explained in the glossary at the back. Likewise, we have avoided abbreviations in these books; the only one used which is not in current everyday English is L1, i.e. the students' mother tongue.

Although all of the ideas in these books are presented in English, you may need to explain or even try some of them, at least initially, in the students' L1. There is nothing wrong with this: L1 can be a useful, efficient resource, especially for explaining methodology. New ideas, which may challenge the traditional methods of teaching and learning, can be very threatening to both teachers and students. So, especially with lower-level classes, you can make them less threatening by translating them. This is not wasting time in the English class, as these ideas will help the students to learn/study more efficiently and learn more English in the long term.

Teaching a mixed-ability class

1 What is a mixed-ability class?

In a sense, every language class in a secondary school can be said to be mixed ability. This is because every class is made up of a group of individuals, and each of those individuals is, to some extent, different in terms of their knowledge and ability. The term 'mixed-ability' is normally used, however, for a group where these individual differences are very pronounced and particularly where there is a marked difference in language level.

To be more specific, mixed-ability refers to:

- classes in which there is a very clear difference in language level among the students. There may be differences in the level of their abilities in the receptive and productive skills, FLUENCY and ACCURACY work, grammatical knowledge, size of vocabulary, command of pronunciation and so on.

- classes in which there are clear differences in learning style, speed and aptitude among the students. Some students seem to be good at languages or perhaps good at all subjects, able to pick things up quickly and remember them, while others are slower, lack study skills and generally experience more difficulties in learning.

- classes in which there are clear differences in the students' background knowledge, knowledge of the world and their skills and talents in other areas. Some of these differences may be linked to age, sex, different levels of maturity, different interests and so on.

- classes in which there are different levels of motivation. Some of the students may have a very positive attitude towards learning English while others may see it as just another school subject.

2 What problems do mixed-ability classes present for the teacher?

Read the comments made by teachers about mixed-ability classes.
- Tick the ones you have experienced.
- Grade the problems, e.g. 1 = very important for me, 2 = quite important for me, 3 = not such a problem for me.

Half the students have finished an exercise when the other half have only just begun.

The stronger students get bored if I spend time explaining to the weaker ones.

We've got a syllabus to get through but most of the students are already behind.

The stronger students dominate.

The weaker students sit at the back and start disrupting the lesson.

The weaker students don't even try.

I don't know where to pitch my lesson.

The weaker students are always asking me things in their own language and want everything explained in it.

Some of the weaker students try so hard but they still get bad marks.

When I'm doing pair or groupwork I don't know whether it's better to put strong and weak students together or put students of the same level in the groups.

Some of the students' written homework is an absolute disaster – grammar, spelling, everything! I don't know where to start correcting it.

Some of the really good students sometimes ask me difficult questions and one even corrected me once!

In the conclusion (PAGE 77) we will return to these problems and see what solutions we have found. The map of the book (PAGE 3) will help you to find areas of interest to read about.

3 Why does the problem exist?

As you are now a teacher of English, this probably means that you were a successful learner of English. Why? By thinking about the things that help people learn, we will also be able to identify possible problem areas for our weaker students.

Which things do you think were important in helping you learn English? Tick as many as you like in the list below. If you think they were **very** important, put two ticks. If you feel that something was not important, leave it blank.

1 You liked your English teacher(s).
2 You thought the subject would be useful to you in the future, e.g. in travelling or in a job.
3 You worked hard at school in all subjects and generally did well.
4 You had English-speaking relatives or people in your family who were interested in Britain or the USA.
5 You found English easy and made good progress.
6 English classes were fun and interesting, and you liked the books you used.
7 Your English teacher(s) taught well.
8 You liked your classmates in the English class.
9 You studied English for many years.
10 You enjoyed reading or seeing films in English.
11 You enjoyed studying the language.
12 You got good marks.

If you can, ask some other adults (or higher-level students in your school) who have studied English (or another foreign language) to answer the questions. Find out if they were successful or unsuccessful learners at school. Are any of the points listed above more important than others?

From the questionnaire, you will have some ideas about why some people are more successful language learners than others and therefore why the problem of mixed-ability classes exists. Here is a summary:

1 Students come from different learning backgrounds

Some may have studied more English at primary level than others. Some may have attended private language schools for extra English. Thus they may have spent different amounts of time studying. Even if they have spent the same amount of time studying, they may have used different coursebooks which covered different ground, or had teachers who emphasised different skills or language areas in their teaching.

2 Students progress at different rates

This is likely to affect classes of students who have already studied some English. It is due to different learning styles and the way students respond to the teacher's style and approach. Some learners may be primarily VISUAL, which means, for example, that they like to see things written down. Others are primarily AUDITORY, which means they learn best and remember things best through listening. Others are KINESTHETIC, which means they like to learn through doing. If the teacher's approaches tended to emphasise the visual element, then it is likely that the primarily visual learners will have progressed at a faster rate.

3 Some students find learning a second language easy and some find it difficult

What exactly constitutes 'learning aptitude' or 'a gift for languages' is not clear but it probably includes things like the ability to:

… perceive and recognise new sounds
… establish sound-symbol relationships
… recognise patterns in language forms and infer rules
… notice similarities and differences in meanings and language forms
… memorise and recall new verbal information.

4 Some students may find formal study easier than others

These students will have adopted good study habits and appropriate learning strategies in all subjects at school. They pay attention and participate in class, they ask questions if they do not understand, they keep neat notebooks and they do their homework conscientiously. Other students do none of these things and seem to make little progress in their learning. There may also be students who experience learning difficulties due to dyslexia, hearing or sight problems.

5 Students may already have a positive or negative attitude

If students have already started studying English, they may have developed a positive or negative attitude towards the language or towards themselves as learners. This may largely depend on how successful they have been or how they have been treated. For example, if they enjoyed the classes, got on well with the other students and had an encouraging teacher, they are likely to have a fairly positive attitude. On the other hand, if they found the classes boring, didn't like the other students and had a teacher who constantly criticised and corrected, they are likely to have developed a negative attitude!

6 There may be other influences

Things other than the students' classroom experiences may have influenced their attitude and ability, e.g. they may have:

… English-speaking family
… travelled to English-speaking countries
… satellite TV, CD-ROM or computers with English programmes at home
… personal interests such as a love of English or American pop music
… an English-speaking penfriend
… a future ambition for a job that involves English.

When you take on a new class you can use a questionnaire to build up a profile of the students. This will give you useful background information. Looking at the above points, what questions could you ask? Think about the students' age and language level. (You might decide to do an activity like this in L1 if the students are beginners.)

Ask the students to do the questionnaire on each other in pairs.

Here is an example of a very simple questionnaire for students who have already studied some English. Another questionnaire designed to focus on attitudes to learning English appears on PHOTOCOPIABLE PAGE 1.

1 How long have you studied English? ....

2 How do you like to learn best?
   – with your eyes? [ ]
   – with your ears? [ ]
   – by doing things? [ ]

3 Did you like your English classes? Why or why not? ....

4 Do you think English is:
   – useful? [ ]
   – interesting? [ ]
   – fun? [ ]

5 What's your English like?
   – very good [ ]
   – OK [ ]
   – not very good [ ]
   – terrible [ ]

6 Do you ever listen to, read, write or speak English outside school? What for? ....

4 How can we deal with mixed-ability classes?

The variety of factors which account for mixed ability among our students means that we need to find a variety of solutions to the problem of dealing with mixed-ability classes.

In **Part A** of this book we will look at ways of **changing**, i.e. ways of trying to ensure that all students have equal opportunities to learn. This means in particular improving opportunities for weaker learners. The first four chapters focus on the following aspects of changing:

Classroom management skills

By effective classroom management skills you can ensure that all learners are involved as much as possible in the lesson.

Motivating students

By trying to ensure that all students are motivated you can improve chances of success in learning.

Catering for different learning styles

By finding out about and trying to cater for different learning styles in the class you can increase learning opportunities for all students.

Learner training

By focusing on learner training you can make students aware of effective learning behaviours and strategies both in and out of class.

These four areas are fundamental in any teaching situation but are even more crucial with a mixed-ability class if all students are to be given equal opportunities to learn.

In **Part B** of the book we look at ways of **coping**, i.e. practical techniques and teaching ideas suitable for a mixed-ability class, linked particularly to the specific problem of mixed levels and learning speeds in one class but also different knowledge of the world and interests. The following areas are covered:

Grading tasks

Students work on the same material but with tasks prepared by the teacher adjusted to different levels of difficulty.

Self access

Students use different materials to practise different language items and skills according to their needs.

Content teaching

Different topics and subjects are introduced into the language class to motivate students and also allow those with different strengths, interests and knowledge of the world to shine.

Activities with different responses

Students are involved in groupwork which requires different responses from different students in order to be completed, thereby catering for mixed levels and varied skills.

Open-ended activities

Students do the same task but can respond at their own level.

Dealing with different learning speeds

Ideas for planning course content, dealing with fast finishers, LOCKSTEP phases of the lesson and homework tasks for weaker and stronger students.

Assessment

Ideas for when and how teachers and the students themselves can evaluate their progress and assess their work.

In the conclusion we will look back at the problems we have identified in teaching mixed-ability classes and see what solutions have been found.

PART A **Changing**

CHAPTER 1

Classroom management

Good classroom management skills are absolutely essential in the mixed-ability class since organising and running our classrooms efficiently and effectively will maximise opportunities for all students to learn.

1 Spread attention

Make sure you involve all the students. It's very easy to let the strong and extrovert students dominate. Make a conscious effort to allow quieter and weaker students the opportunity to participate by:
… establishing eye contact
… not allowing weaker students to hide at the back
… nominating weaker students to answer easier questions
… checking they have understood instructions
… monitoring during pair and groupwork.

2 Learn and use students' names

This will help to make students feel recognised as individuals and make them feel more involved. There are many activities to help you to get to know names when you meet a new class. Here are two ideas:

Alphabetical order

- Tell the students they have to organise themselves either by standing in a line or sitting at their desks in alphabetical order, according to their first names.
- Give them an example: write some names on the board and ask which should be first, second and so on.
- Elicit from them what question they will have to ask their classmates: *What's your name?* and drill it if necessary.
- Tell them where the first student should sit or stand and where the last student should be.
- Then the students stand up, find out their classmates' names and sit or stand in the right place.
- When they are settled, go round the class in order, getting them to say their names out loud so that everyone can check if the order is correct.

Throw the ball

- Hold the ball up and say your name, pointing at yourself.
- Then throw it to a student and ask the student to say his/her name.
- This student then throws it to another student who says his/her name.

- This continues until all the students have said their names, then the students can throw the ball again, but saying the recipient's name first.

3 The teacher's attitude

Think back to good and bad teachers from your past. Characteristics often attributed to good teachers are:
bright, cheerful and friendly   organised   fair   confident   authoritative (but not authoritarian)   enthusiastic   encouraging

Can you add to the list?

Many people claim that the teacher was a key influence on their liking of and their success in different subjects at school. It may have been one of the factors that you identified as important in your own learning of English in the introduction. It is worth reflecting on the impression you create as a teacher and trying to cultivate the above qualities.

4 Praise and encouragement

Students need to feel noticed but also valued. Recognising good behaviour, effort and good work is important. Say *good* and *well done*, smile and nod to express approval in class. In responding to written work, don't just focus on the errors but comment on what is good. With behaviour in class, reward what is good rather than punish what is bad. For example, if students are working in groups and there is just one group chatting or not doing what they should, it is better to draw attention to and comment positively on those groups who **are** working well rather than the one that is not.

5 Teacher talk

As a teacher, you need to use your voice a lot and how you do this is important. Everybody needs to be able to hear you, otherwise students sitting at the back of the class will stop paying attention. To maintain interest, you also need to vary your voice in terms of tone and pitch. Students also need to be able to recognise signals you use for, e.g. finishing activities and calling their attention. This can be done effectively by simple marker expressions, such as *OK, everybody* and varying the pitch.

Another aspect of teacher talk is grading and relevance. Many teachers have a tendency to talk too much. Teacher talk is fine as long as it is meaningful and comprehensible; if it is in English, it provides useful exposure for the students. Long, overcomplicated and boring explanations of, e.g. a grammar point are not useful and will alienate weaker or unmotivated students in particular. Keep your language simple and pause often to allow students some thinking time.

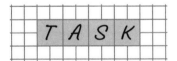

Try video or tape recording (part of) one of your lessons, where you know you will be talking. When you listen to the tape:

Try to decide if what you say is clear and well graded or if it could be confusing. Is there too much teacher talk? Is it too fast or too slow? How much do you think your weaker students could understand? Could you help them more? Could any of the things you said be better phrased?

Think also about your voice quality. Do you sound interesting? Do you vary your pitch?

Is it clear when you want to get the students' attention? What marker expressions do you use? Were they effective?

6 Managing learning activities

Good management of learning activities ensures that all students, however weak or strong, are involved in the lesson.

Focus on instructions

- Plan your instructions in advance; decide exactly what you need to tell the students and how you will say it. Keep the language as simple as possible and the instructions as short as possible.
- Make sure you have everyone's attention before giving the instructions.
- Make sure you look at the students as you give instructions; use the board to give examples, hold up the handout and point at it, demonstrate the activity with one of the stronger students if it helps.
- Use gestures to support what you are saying. For example, if the students have to close their books, you can demonstrate this, or if they must not show their worksheet to their partner, demonstrate this by holding it close to you with an arm round it.
- Pause as you give instructions; if the students look confused, try repeating or paraphrasing what you have just said.
- Check your instructions by asking check questions, e.g. *What do you do first? Then?* or by getting the students to repeat the instructions in their own words.
- Give out handouts or materials to the students **after** they have understood what to do. If you give them out before, students often start reading and don't listen to the instructions.
- Sometimes written instructions may be more appropriate. If so, give students time to read them and check in pairs that they understand what to do. Then ask a few check questions (e.g. *Are you going to work alone? Are you going to write or speak?*) or get them to repeat the instructions in their own words.
- It is often a good idea to do a couple of examples with the whole class before they start working individually, or in pairs or groups.

Use pair and groupwork

These are essential techniques in the mixed-ability class.

- Weaker students are more likely to participate in small groups.
- They are more likely to ask questions about things they don't understand.
- Students are more likely to help each other.
- There is more practice time for everyone.
- The teacher can help those students who need it more easily.
- Students take on more responsibility for their own learning and have to think.
- Dominant students can only dominate a few of the students at a time.
- Students can assume different roles according to their level.

This means that part of your instructions will often include grouping the students. You need to decide how this will be done too.

- Do you want mixed groupings of students or students of equal levels of ability for the task? This is important because, as we shall see in Part B, there are some activities which should be done with students grouped according to level and others in which they need to be mixed, so when you meet a new class you need to devise some activities and perhaps a test to give you a clear idea of each student's level.

◆ FOR MORE ON ASSESSMENT, SEE CHAPTER 11

- How can you manage the grouping smoothly? Coloured cards or CUISENAIRE RODS, numbers or names can be useful. For example, if you want your class of 32 divided into eight groups, you will need pieces of card in eight different colours. Cut up enough pieces of card for each member of the class to have one. Decide who you want to work together and give them pieces of the same colour. When they have their card, tell them to group together with all the students who have cards of the same colour.

- Alternatively, give each student one of eight names (strawberry, orange, mango, etc. or camel, giraffe, elephant, etc.) or numbers (1 to 8) and then tell them to get together with the students with the same name or number.

Set a time limit for the activity before the students begin

Keep to the time you have set and warn students about two minutes before the end, e.g. *You have two more minutes, then you must stop.* Give a clear signal that everyone is to stop even if they have not quite finished: *OK, everybody, now stop.*

Monitor while the students are working

This means going round helping or noting problem areas and answering students' questions. Try to see as many groups as possible. Go to those students who are likely to have more difficulty first to ensure they have started on the right track. Monitoring also enables you to know when to stop the activity. Students are likely to finish at different times. It depends on the activity (if it is absolutely necessary that everybody finishes this one before beginning the next) but in many cases it is probably best to stop it when most, rather than all, the students have finished.

Find things to do with fast finishers

This problem is examined and ideas are given in Chapter 10, page 68.

Make sure everyone benefits from feedback

If a whole-class feedback stage is necessary, check that everyone has heard and understood the answers and has corrected their work. Self-checking against a key or checking in mixed-level pairs or groups may be more useful. When you monitor, focus on those students who experienced most difficulty during the task.

7 Using the board

It is essential that all the students can see and read what you write on the board, whether it is vocabulary, prompts for an activity or a record of the lesson. If some of them can't, they will either not bother to copy, copy wrongly or not do the activity. It is likely to be the weaker students who have more difficulty if your boardwork is unclear and they will get left behind again.

When you write on the board:

- check it is clear and legible. Is your writing big enough to be seen from the back of the class? Stand at the back of the class occasionally to check.

- organise it clearly. It is a good idea to keep a column on one side of the board for items of vocabulary that come up in class. Planning your main boardwork is essential since this will provide a record of the lesson for the students.

- give clear instructions. Do the students copy what is written or just read it?

- if they are copying, give them enough time to do so. Go round and monitor, paying particular attention to the weaker students or the careless copiers.

- encourage everyone to check their work. They can also check their partner's work.

T A S K

Cover the key below. Look at this piece of boardwork from a lesson.
What is wrong with it? How would you improve it?

Rabbits live underground   They does~~nt~~

He LIVES   where   sheeps
        birds
mouse — mice   COWS   Austrelia
        They live in

Compare your ideas with the board plan and notes below.

Where do they live ?

Birds live in ┊ nests.
            ┊ cages.

Kangaroos live in Australia.

Rabbits live underground.

Sheep ┊ live in fields.
Cows ┊

| 1 | 2 |
| mouse | mice |

to build a nest

a Kangaroo

1 sheep, 2 sheep

Problems with first board

It's a mixture of capitals and lower case.
Some words are illegible.
There are some spelling mistakes.
The sentences are incomplete.
There's no topic heading.
There's no indication of parts of speech.
It's disorganised and messy.

Better on second board

The board is organised, with a separate column for vocabulary.
The sentences/phrases are complete and students can see the parts of speech.
The handwriting is clear.
Lots of help with grammar is given.

8 Classroom layout

The way that the classroom is organised and the use that both you and your students make of the space available has a powerful influence on classroom dynamics and learning potential. If your classroom is badly laid out and neither you nor the students ever move, some students will soon stop paying attention. The problems of the mixed-ability class will be made worse.

There are various layouts possible with large classes, such as:

1 Students in pairs at desks
2 Students sitting either side of a horseshoe of tables
3 Students in groups around tables

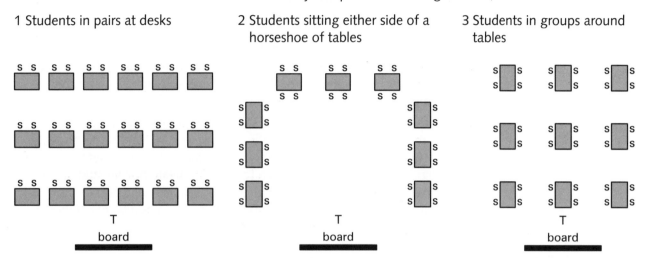

Depending on the activity you are doing, some layouts may be better than others. However, it is not often practical or possible to move the furniture every time you change activity. So you need to choose which layout suits you best. If other colleagues use the same room, any changes would have to be done in consultation with them, of course.

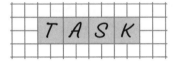

TASK

If your classroom layout is not one of the above, draw a plan of it. Now look at the possible classroom layouts and decide:

Can the teacher see everyone and move around easily to monitor students?

Can the students work easily individually/in pairs/in groups? Can they see the teacher, the board and each other? Can they stand up and move around easily?

If the answer to most of these questions is *yes*, then your classroom layout is probably all right. If the answer is *no*, think about how you could improve it.

If you really cannot move the desks because of school regulations or other teachers, and you are not happy with the layout, then remember that moving chairs, students and yourself is much easier and may solve the problems.

Remember that with a mixed-ability class, it is particularly important:

… to ensure that everyone can see you and be seen

… to vary interaction (whole class, individual, pairs, groups)

… for you to move around to monitor at appropriate times

… for the students to move around, to work in different groupings for different activities and to do some activities on their feet.

TASK

Look back at the areas discussed in this chapter about classroom management. Are there any areas that you could improve upon?

CHAPTER 2

Motivating students

Motivation is an essential factor affecting learning. In a mixed-ability class, the weaker learners are often those with least motivation. Their motivation is often reduced further by the sense of failure as they find the subject difficult and make little progress. Successful learners, on the other hand, are often those who are more motivated from the beginning and their sense of success further motivates them. It is therefore very important that in a mixed-ability class the teacher works on motivating all the students.

For many children, the main reason for studying English is that it is part of the school syllabus. This is not very motivating as a reason in itself. Some students, those with English-speaking family, for example, may have more positive reasons for learning. It is up to the teacher then to try to motivate his/her students, to show them that English is not 'just another school subject' and also to show them that it is interesting and relevant to them. It should also be remembered that enjoyment can be a powerful motivator.

1 How useful is English?

Raising students' awareness of just how much English there is around them, how many people speak English, and how much English they have already met can increase motivation. These activities can be done just as well by weaker students as by stronger ones but are best done in mixed-level groups.

Proper names

The students list names of:
… bands or singers they like who sing in English
… famous English-speaking people (sportsmen, politicians, writers, film stars, etc.)
… films and TV programmes they have seen.

Countries

The students find out which countries have English as a first language. Alternatively, provide a map with the countries marked on and get the students to name them.

English around me

The students bring in any examples of English texts they can find, e.g. food wrappers, names of shops or films, titles or words of pop songs, instructions on domestic appliances. They make a wall poster or make a page in their own files or notebooks. This can be added to as the students find more examples.

English and my language

The students brainstorm all the words they already know which are used in both their language and in English, e.g. *stop, hotel, taxi, cafe, bar, pizza, TV, radio*. Provide picture prompts to help the students. Again this can be made into a wall poster or a page in the students' own notebooks.

◆ SEE PHOTOCOPIABLE PAGE 2

Words I already know

As an extension or alternative to the above activity the students can brainstorm all the English words they already know, e.g. *love, hard rock, music, tea*.

English and jobs

Get the students to put a list of jobs in order of how important English is to each one. Get them to compare and justify their ideas in groups. The students can do this in L1 but using the English names for the jobs, e.g.

pop singer	footballer	model	politician	secretary
English teacher	computer programmer		hotel manager	
businessman	flight attendant	shopkeeper	doctor	

The students can then say which jobs they would most/least like to do and why.

Survey

The students interview some adults (e.g. parents, other teachers, friends of the family, etc.) about their jobs and if they use English or not. This can be done in L1, of course. The questions they ask are: *What is your job? Do you use English at all? Do you think English can be useful in your professional area?*

Then they report back to the class about their findings. Many adults will – hopefully! – say that English is or would be useful to them so this may make less motivated students more aware of the 'real life' advantages of the language.

2 Creating an English environment

If it is possible in your school, try to create an English classroom. If this is not possible, then an English noticeboard with changing displays could be set up somewhere in the school. The following displays can help in creating a visually interesting and motivating environment:

… posters of Britain or other English-speaking countries
… posters the students make/displays of their work
… pictures of famous English-speaking people with speech bubbles the students have made
… English cartoons/signs.

Each week a different class can be responsible for organising the display. A corner with English books, comics, magazines and games is also a good idea if you have the space, or you could have a portable box of these things which can be used at the beginning and end of lessons and for fast finishers.

3 Creating a good atmosphere

A good classroom atmosphere is important in terms of motivation and morale. It is very important with a mixed-ability class that the teacher encourages an atmosphere of co-operation, tolerance and mutual support. If students feel comfortable in a group they will be more open to learning and may develop a more positive attitude towards the language they are studying.

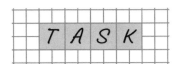

What do you do to help promote a good learning atmosphere in your classes? Make a list of things that you do in order to create a sense of group cohesion and a positive learning atmosphere in your classes.

Then compare your ideas with the suggestions below.

Make a class contract which everyone signs.

There are different ways of doing this but it is best if the 'rules' come primarily from the students themselves rather than from you. Here is a suggested procedure for students who have not done a class contract before.

- Show the students signs which express rules. Get them in pairs or small groups to identify what they mean and where they might see them. If the students are beginners they can do this in L1, but it is a useful opportunity for you to feed in some vocabulary at the feedback stage. Here are some examples.

- Ask the students to say why these rules exist and which they think are good or bad rules.
- Ask them to list some school rules and say why these exist.
- Tell them to think about their English class and brainstorm rules they think are a good idea. To start them off, elicit and feed in ideas such as:
  Students should try to speak English whenever they can.
  The teacher should be patient with the students when they make mistakes.
  Students should show respect to each other.
  The teacher should make his/her lessons interesting.
  Let them work in groups, perhaps making up five rules for the teacher and five for the students. Then as a whole class, elicit their ideas and get the class to agree on the best rules; if it is necessary, you can have some influence here to make sure things you think are important are included!
- Once the contract is agreed and written up, it should be signed by everyone.

A class contract can help foster a sense of class identity, a sense of 'justice' and a clear reference point when rules are broken.

Example of a class contract

We, the students, promise to
- speak English as much as we can
- be polite to each other and to the teacher
- do our homework on time
- put chewing gum in the bin before the lesson
- write neatly in our notebooks
- bring our books to class
The teacher promises to
- make our lessons interesting
- be fair to everyone
- help us to be good students of English
Signed ...

(This procedure is based on the one given in *Teaching Teenagers* by Herbert Puchta and Michael Schratz, Addison-Wesley Longman, 1993.)

Be fair and don't discriminate

Even if there are students you prefer, you should never show this. Children and teenagers have a very strong sense of what is and is not fair and will easily identify instances of favouritism or discrimination. Show an equal amount of interest in all students, e.g. by spreading attention, learning and using names, individual counselling and so on.

Provide opportunities for learners to get to know each other

Personalisation activities are important here, i.e. practice activities which enable students to use English to talk or write about themselves. ◆ SEE PAGE 21 Also, by changing seating arrangements and groupings you can discourage the formation of fixed groups or cliques, though you will almost certainly find that some groupings work better than others in the end. It is essential in a mixed-ability group that you encourage tolerance and co-operation. You should immediately condemn any behaviour such as laughing at the weaker students, referring back to the class contract if necessary.

Encourage and train students to listen to each other

This is part of showing each other respect.

- If one student is giving you an answer to a question, encourage the others to listen by asking them if they agree afterwards.

- Make students aware of active listening strategies. Tell one student (A) to talk for one minute on a chosen subject (in L1 if necessary). Give a secret instruction to their partner (B) to show no interest at all. Afterwards ask A to say what B did (yawned, drummed their fingers, looked around the room, etc.) and how A felt. Elicit how we show interest when we are listening: by eye contact, making noises (e.g. *mmm, really*), facial expressions, etc. Then get students to practise listening and showing interest.

- If one student or a group of students is giving a presentation to the class, make sure you set a task for the listeners so that they have a reason to listen. This might be as simple as thinking of two questions to ask at the end.

Have some 'class' activities

- The students produce a poster about important events in the lives of the class members, e.g.

> 1986   Fifteen of us were born.
> 1987   Twenty-five of us were born.
> 1988   Juan's brother was born.
>   Carmen moved to Madrid.
> 1989   Sofia broke her leg.

- The students produce a fact sheet about the class. Copy and cut up PHOTOCOPIABLE PAGE 3 to give one question to each student/pair. All the students/pairs ask everyone the same question and keep a note of the answer. They can then produce a list of facts about the class. With a large class students can work in groups, each student asking two or three questions. When all the students have questioned members of their group, they get together with other students who asked the same question to their groups and add their results together. They then write a sentence onto a large card or a poster, e.g.

Twenty of us have sisters.

Nine of us can rollerskate.

Twelve of us walk to school.

All of us except Antonia and Maria like hamburgers.

Sixteen of us have a pet.

You can adjust this activity to different levels by choosing carefully the structures you use. In the photocopiable prompts the structures used for the first prompt cards are simpler than those used at the end.

- Get the students to do class surveys, about, e.g. likes and dislikes, eating habits, pets, holidays. With the information they gather they then produce a graph, table or pie chart, or write up an article based on the information gathered.

Don't compare students' performances

Competition in games and quizzes can be motivating but you should never encourage a sense of competition in grades. This may motivate stronger students who are competing for top position but will probably demotivate everyone else.

4 The lesson

Even if the students don't have any particular external motivation for learning English, the fact of enjoying the lessons themselves can provide powerful motivation. How can you make lessons motivating?

- Make the lessons interesting in terms of content and topic: find out what topics students are interested in outside the classroom.
- Include plenty of variety in terms of activity, e.g. don't always use the coursebook, and ensure that the pace of your lesson is balanced.
- Balance 'serious' activities with more 'fun' ones: too many games are as bad as too many dull exercises in the classroom. Laughter is important but so are concentration and quieter times.
- Vary the emphasis from ACCURACY to FLUENCY: if you do some accuracy work, use the rest of the lesson or the next lesson for some fluency work.
- Provide a balance of skills work: use reading, listening, speaking and writing activities in more or less equal amounts.
- Vary the way you do things and the tasks students do, i.e. don't always follow the same procedure when presenting grammar or doing a reading comprehension.
- Be sensitive to the students' moods and be flexible to avoid being boring: this may mean adapting something you have planned if it is not working.
- Cater for different learning styles and preferences. ◆ SEE CHAPTER 3
- Include specific activities that cater for mixed levels.
- Introduce student choice when possible, e.g. in terms of choosing projects, readers, or the order in which you tackle the activities in the coursebook.
- Introduce opportunities for creativity and things which appeal to children's or teenagers' imaginations, e.g. rather than using dull, faceless, coursebook characters to introduce family vocabulary, use the Addams family or one of your own creation. Things which are funny, strange or moving in some other way will be more memorable than things which are everyday and ordinary.

Many of the points mentioned above mean that you will have to use the coursebook quite judiciously, that is, you will need to select, adapt and omit activities rather than using it as it stands.

Look back at your records of work from a recent series of lessons with a mixed-ability class. How far do you think the lessons followed the recommendations above? Which ideas could you introduce to make your lessons more motivating for the students?

5 Personalisation

Relating the language to the students themselves is important as this will make the language more meaningful and memorable for all of them. You can personalise any new language. Here are some examples.

Vocabulary of animals

Put the list of animals in order according to:
a) how much you like them
b) how much you'd like one as a pet
c) how much you'd like to be one.

Vocabulary of the house

a) Draw a plan of your room with its furniture and label it.
b) Draw and describe or label your ideal room.

Past simple

a) Describe a memorable day in your life.
b) Describe what you did last weekend/last holidays, etc.

Have got

a) What have you got in your schoolbag? (pockets/bedroom)
b) How many teeth/scars/long fingernails/fillings have you got?
c) Write three true sentences and three false sentences about yourself using *I've got*. Read them out to the other students, who guess which are true and which are false.
d) Find someone who ...

   ... has got a twin   ... has got a computer
   ... has got a bicycle   ... has got two or more cousins.

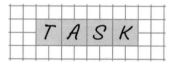

Cover the ideas below then devise ways of personalising the following language points.
1 clothes vocabulary   2 *can* for ability
Now look at these ideas. Did you think of any of them?

1 clothes vocabulary
  a) Describe what you are wearing now.
  b) Imagine you are in these situations. What are you wearing?
    You are meeting the queen/president.
    You are at a disco.
    You are playing your favourite sport.
    You are painting your bedroom.
  c) What are your favourite clothes?

2 *can* for ability
  a) True and false sentences about what you can do.
  b) Find someone who ...

    ... can play the piano   ... can make a cake
    ... can sing a song in English   ... can swim.

◆ SEE PAGE 59 FOR INSTRUCTIONS FOR THIS ACTIVITY

  c) Imagine you are the following. What can you do? What can't you do?

    a kangaroo   a fish   an alarm clock   a telephone   a robot
    a refrigerator

CHAPTER 3

Catering for different types of learner

If students enjoy their English lessons, this can provide powerful motivation. Ensuring that lessons are well paced and contain different kinds of activity will keep students interested. It is also important that you cater for different kinds of learner. Learners have different learning styles and preferences; if you cater only for one type of learner, then the others will fall behind. The important point here is variety in terms of your approach to learning activities.

1 What different kinds of learners are there?

There is no simple answer to this but research has shown that people do learn in different ways. Different types of learner have been identified according to which sense they seem to favour for learning and remembering.

Visual learners

VISUAL LEARNERS like to have visual cues. For example, they prefer reading instructions to listening to them because they understand and remember them better, and they prefer looking at their coursebook to listening to explanations.

Auditory learners

AUDITORY LEARNERS learn and remember better when they listen. Thus they prefer the teacher to give oral instructions and they remember things they have listened to more easily than things they have read.

Kinesthetic learners

KINESTHETIC LEARNERS prefer to learn by doing or by experience. They prefer demonstration to written or verbal explanations. They will learn better by being actively involved in a task, by acting, drawing or making something.

Other classifications of learning styles focus on how students like to learn.

Individual learners

These learners prefer to study alone because it helps them remember and they feel they work more efficiently.

Group learners

These learners remember more and work more efficiently when they work with other people.

Concrete learners

CONCRETE LEARNERS like visual and verbal experiences and they dislike routine learning and written work. They like to be entertained and physically involved; they want immediate, varied and lively learning experiences.

Analytical learners

ANALYTICAL LEARNERS are independent learners who like problem solving and working things out for themselves. They like new learning material to be presented systematically and logically and they like to follow up on their own. They are serious and hardworking, and are badly affected by failure.

Communicative learners

COMMUNICATIVE LEARNERS like a social approach to learning. They learn well from discussion and group activities, and need personal feedback and interaction. They get on best in a democratically run class.

Authority-oriented learners

AUTHORITY-ORIENTED LEARNERS relate well to a traditional classroom, preferring the teacher as an authority figure. They like clear instructions and they need structure and logical progression in what they learn.

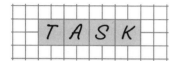

T A S K

Think about your students. Do any of them fit into the categories of learner types listed above? Do you cater enough for them in your classes?

2 How can you find out about students' preferred learning styles?

We do not need to worry about precise classification of our learners but we do need to find out something about their learning style and preferences for:
… particular kinds of classroom activities
… teacher behaviour
… grouping arrangements
… sensory modes.

This kind of information may help us to predict what will and will not work in our classes. In doing the task above you may have found you have a few ideas about some of your students but not all of them. Here are some ideas for finding out about your students' preferred learning styles more systematically:

Questionnaires

You can use a questionnaire to find out about students' attitudes to different ways of learning. You can do this at the beginning of the year or after you have been teaching a group for a while and they have experienced different approaches. PHOTOCOPIABLE PAGE 4 gives a pictorial questionnaire which you can use at a very low level. You can, of course, do the same with statements in L1, e.g.

> *How do you like to learn? Tick the statements that are true for you:*
>
> *1 I prefer working alone to working in a group.*
> *2 I remember things better when I see them written down.*
> *3 I like the teacher to correct all my mistakes.*

When you have done the questionnaires you will need to analyse them. Are there any general tendencies in the class? Or is there great variety among individuals? General tendencies may mean that you should favour some teaching approaches over others whereas a lot of variation in the student responses may suggest that a more varied approach is better. If you return the questionnaires to the students, keep a note of their responses for future reference.

Student feedback

You can ask students what they thought of particular activities after they have done them. This can form part of their work record: in the last five minutes of the lesson the students complete a form saying what they learned or practised, how they did it, what they liked and what they did not like. There is an example of a work record sheet on PHOTOCOPIABLE PAGE 5.

Formal and informal testing

You will be able to assess the effectiveness of the learning activities you use by evaluating student progress, both through informal checking and formal tests. Different students may remember different things if they have very different learning preferences but if there are some lessons that no one seems to remember well, this may indicate a general tendency in the class.

3 How can you cater for different learning styles?

It is almost certainly the case that some learners have traditionally been at an advantage in the classroom. VISUAL LEARNERS, individual learners and AUTHORITY-ORIENTED LEARNERS have been favoured, particularly in secondary school, since much teaching has depended on the written word, individual work and the teacher in a traditional authoritarian role.

The teacher's own learning style and preferences may influence his/her teaching style. So if you are the type of learner described above (and it seems that many teachers are!), then your teaching style is likely to reflect this.

Obviously, other types of learner will then be at a disadvantage because they do not learn well in this way. Thus they may fall behind. It is important, therefore, to make a conscious effort to vary the teaching approaches you use, so that you cater for as many types of learner as possible.

We will look now at some different ways of approaching various learning activities to ensure that we cater for different types of learner.

Grammar presentation

TASK

Cover the ideas below. You want to present the present simple with *he/she* for talking about daily routines. How many different ways can you think of doing this? Which learning styles does each one seem suitable for?

Now read the following ideas and compare them with your own.

- Use pictures of a character, e.g. Dracula, a famous footballer or pop star, etc. (depending on the students' ages and interests) doing a variety of actions with a time next to each one. Hold the pictures up and try to elicit the language from the students. If they don't know how to say it, you tell them. Model it clearly, using your fingers to help if necessary to indicate each word, and get the students to repeat. Go through the pictures one by one, modelling and drilling. Recap on them orally before you write them up on the board at the end.

  This approach is likely to appeal to students who like to learn by listening and repeating, that is AUDITORY LEARNERS. It may also appeal to CONCRETE LEARNERS who enjoy visual and verbal experiences.

- Give each pair or group of students a set of sentences describing someone's day, written on separate strips of card. Give them another set of cards with times on (e.g. *at 7.00*) They match them up and put them in order as best they can. You then play a tape or read out the correct version. Students listen and correct their sentences as necessary. Then they copy them into their notebooks.

  This approach is more suitable for VISUAL and KINESTHETIC LEARNERS since the written word is used and the students are involved in a task. Students who like working in groups also benefit as may ANALYTICAL and COMMUNICATIVE LEARNERS.

- Put a picture of a person on the board and draw a clock, giving a certain time. Mime the activity, e.g. *Dracula wakes up at midnight*. As you mime, say the sentence and repeat it several times. At this stage the students only listen. After listening to all the sentences, tell the students to mime as you go through them again. First, you mime with them, then let them mime on their own. You can then say the sentences in a different order and get the students to do the right mime. You then mime and get the students to say the sentences together. After this, ask individuals to say the sentences while the other students mime. Finally, show the students the sentences written on large cards; they read and mime.

This approach will appeal to KINESTHETIC LEARNERS who learn by doing, AUDITORY LEARNERS as the language is first spoken, and CONCRETE LEARNERS who enjoy physical involvement and lively learning experiences.

- Write some example sentences on the board and ask the students to translate them. Name the tense, explain its use and underline the -*s* at the end of the verb. The students copy the example sentences and the grammar explanation into their notebooks.

This approach is likely to suit VISUAL LEARNERS, who like to see things written down, individual learners, and AUTHORITY-ORIENTED LEARNERS since the teacher is taking a more traditional role as instructor.

The four examples above are all valid ways of presenting this piece of new language and you probably came up with more good ideas of your own. As we have seen, different approaches will suit different types of learner.

Taking into consideration all of the different classifications of types of learner, the following factors seem to be the important things that we can vary in our approaches to teaching grammar:

… the type of prompts and aids used (written, visual, oral, acted out)

… interaction: individual, whole-class or groupwork or pairwork

… students can be told the rules, given a model or asked to work things out for themselves

… examples and practice before rules or vice versa

… student roles, degree and type of participation

… type of student response, i.e. oral, written, acting out.

By varying the approach you use for presentations and using different approaches when recycling grammar, you will be catering for different learner types in a mixed-ability class.

Vocabulary

There are a lot of different ways of presenting and practising vocabulary, too. By varying the type of learning activity, you can cater for different learning styles and help make the vocabulary more memorable.

Think of as many ways as you can of presenting the following vocabulary items. Use the list on page 26 to help you.

1 parts of the body

2 a set of action verbs: *run, ride a horse, swim, ride a bike, climb a tree, play football*

Here are some ideas to start with:

a) noises on tape
b) pictures to elicit the words orally
c) matching words to situations, definitions or pictures
d) picture dictionaries
e) translation
f) mime or gesture
g) a text with gaps and a list of the words

1 parts of the body

- Point to different parts of your body and say the word, e.g. *foot*. Repeat this, getting students to point to their feet. Do it a third time while the students say the words in chorus. Then give a student one of the other 'body parts' words on card; he/she says it out loud and the other students point.

- Give students a picture of a body and a jumbled list of the words for parts of the body. In pairs they match them.

- In groups, students draw a picture of a body on a poster. Then give them the words for parts of the body on cards; they stick them in the right place.

- Give students a list of the English words for parts of the body and a list of the words in L1. They use a dictionary and work individually to match them.

2 a set of action verbs

- Give the students sentences with gaps and pictures next to them; they have to choose the correct verb to complete the sentence.

- Mime and elicit the verbs, then students mime them.

- Show the students pictures of the actions and try to elicit the verbs orally .

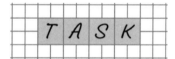

Go through the activities presented in the section on Vocabulary above and work out which type(s) of learner each activity would suit.

Skills work

It is also important to provide practice in all the four skills so that different types of learner are catered for. For example, if you do a lot of silent reading and writing in class and little listening and oral work you are favouring VISUAL LEARNERS over AUDITORY LEARNERS. Thus you need to ensure that you include a good balance of the skills.

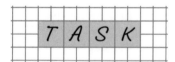

Can you think of some ideas for varying work on the productive skills (speaking and writing) and the receptive skills (reading and listening) so that you cater for different types of learner? Think about how you could vary interaction, the types of prompts you use and the actual tasks.

Compare your ideas with those in the menu below and on page 27.

Interaction
individual
pairwork   } sitting, standing, mingling
groupwork
whole class

Prompts
written prompts (sentences, words)
pictures (drawings, photographs, magazine pictures)
videos
reading texts (letters, postcards, stories, adverts, magazine articles, headlines,
    newspaper articles, cartoons, instructions, lists, poems, dialogues, plays, recipes, jokes)
listening texts (songs, conversations, adverts, radio programmes, telephone
    conversations, poems, stories, plays, jokes)
noises on tape
music
real objects
CUISENAIRE RODS

Tasks
before language focus, students experiment with language
after language focus, students practise what they have learned

Speaking	**Writing**
discussion	lists (shopping lists, holiday lists)
ROLEPLAY	messages
storytelling	stories
giving instructions to make or do something	poems
talking about oneself	for and against compositions
describe and draw	captions for pictures or strip cartoons
describe and arrange	postcards and letters
find the differences	instructions for doing or making
plays and sketches	something
problem solving	sketches and dialogues
presentations	

Listening and reading
answering written questions (*wh-* questions, true/false, multiple choice)
answering oral questions
ordering pictures
selecting picture(s)
drawing
making something
ordering text
moving/miming
acting out
reading aloud or singing
reading and listening at the same time
gap-filling
choosing titles
labelling a picture or diagram

By varying the types of tasks and activities we use as well as the stage of the
lesson at which we use them and the interaction patterns, we should be able to
cater for different learning styles and preferences and thus maximise
opportunities for all our students to learn.

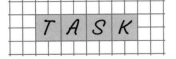

Think back to some skills lessons you have done recently and look at the
suggestions for varying your approaches above. How many different options
have you used? Have you tended to cater for particular learning styles and
preferences? Where could you introduce more variety in future?

CHAPTER 4

Learner training

Some students automatically adopt good learning habits. They:
... pay attention in class and participate
... keep neat notebooks
... do their homework
... carry out learning tasks efficiently and effectively by employing appropriate strategies
... make progress in the language
... know what their strengths and weaknesses are
... know how to try to improve.

In other words, they know how to learn. Not all good language learners do the same things to help them learn, but they find things that work for them. It is absolutely essential in the mixed-ability class that all students are given help to develop good learning habits. If they are not helped, then learners who have not adopted good learning habits will fall further behind and the problem of differences in level will become worse.

Learner training raises students' awareness of how they learn and what they can do to help themselves. It also encourages them to take on more responsibility for their own learning. This in turn will help to equip them for learning beyond the classroom. There are many ways in which you can help your students become better learners.

1 Participation

It is important that learners are involved in the class. Often, weaker learners may lose concentration easily. You can encourage participation by good classroom management skills as we have seen in Chapter 3.

Also, activities which aim to increase student motivation and which cater for different learning styles are essential in encouraging student involvement.

Here are some more ideas for encouraging active participation:

- Give students management responsibilities, e.g. writing the date on the board at the beginning of the lesson, handing out books or papers, cleaning the board at the end of the lesson. Involving the students in this way gives them a sense of ownership of the classroom and a sense of self worth. In particular, it is a way of encouraging weaker learners to take an active role in the class as they can do these tasks just as well as the stronger students.

- When students are working in groups, appoint a group monitor. It is the monitor's responsibility to ensure that English is used and not L1 (if the task is supposed to be done in English), that everyone participates and that the task is completed satisfactorily.

- Teach the students classroom language. This can be done in the beginning by getting students to match English phrases to the L1 equivalents. At the feedback stage, model and drill each expression. Teach them expressions such as:

I'm sorry, I don't understand.
I don't know.
Can you say that again, please?
How do you say ... in English?
What does ... mean?

How do you spell …?
What's the answer to number …?

Display classroom language on the classroom wall if possible so that it can be referred to as necessary. If it cannot be left up on the wall, it can be written on posters which you can carry with you. The students can also have a special section of their notebooks reserved for classroom language which they can refer to. Add to classroom language throughout the course. For example, before doing a pairwork checking task you may want to teach other phrases, such as:

What did you put for number …?
It's your go./You do the next one.
I don't think that's right.
I put the same as you.

By leaving the phrases on the board as students do the activity, the weaker students in particular have something to refer to and can say something.

- Display students' work with their names clearly visible. This can be work produced by a group or by individuals. Encouraging a sense of pride in their work can help motivate all students to produce something good.

- Lesson summary sheets can also provide an incentive to students to participate.

  What did I learn today?
  How much English did I speak?
  How much English did I write?
  Did I concentrate for the whole lesson?

2 Organising notebooks

Good learners keep well organised notebooks or files. It is important that you encourage and train weaker students to do the same as they can use these notes outside class to help them catch up. Again, there are certain aspects of classroom management which are important:

- Good boardwork. What you write should be complete, clear and legible, and the students should also know what and when they are to copy. They need sufficient time to copy, and they should be told to check what they have written and what their partner has written. You should also monitor, paying attention to poor copiers in particular. ◆ SEE CHAPTER 1 PAGE 14

- Help them to organise their notes. If they have ringbinders to put photocopies in, always put holes in the photocopies for them so they can be filed away immediately. If they don't, make sure that any loose handouts for them to keep are pasted into their notebooks. Suggest how they should organise their notes, e.g. chronological order or according to topic. Make the topic or objectives of each lesson clear and make sure they copy this into their notes.

- Look at their notebooks or files on a regular basis and give them a mark or comment for organisation and presentation.

- Separate vocabulary notebooks are very useful and you can help students organise these. Use different ways of organising vocabulary notes when you present new vocabulary to the students and encourage them to transfer new vocabulary from their class notes or from their coursebook into their vocabulary book. Use copies of PHOTOCOPIABLE PAGE 6 to show students different ways of recording vocabulary.

3 Training in using reference books

Students can help themselves by using reference books such as their coursebook, picture dictionaries, bilingual (and monolingual) dictionaries and grammar books. Good learners may automatically make use of these resources but weaker ones may not, so it is important that you raise students' awareness of the advantages of and basic techniques for using them.

The easiest way to do this is by introducing tasks into the classroom that require the students to use these resources, either to do the task in the first place or to check a task they have done. For example, encourage students to check the spelling of words in their dictionaries and train them in using workbook or grammar book keys (if available) to check their own or their partner's work.

Here are some examples of tasks for getting students used to using reference books:

- For getting to know the coursebook and training in scanning skills, give them a list of questions and ask them to find the answers as quickly as possible, e.g.

  Where can you find a summary of the present simple?
  Which unit is about animals?
  Where is the grammar summary for each unit?

- Give students a list of words in L1 on a certain topic, then get them to use a picture dictionary to find the English equivalents.

- Give students a list of English words spelt wrongly. They have to use a dictionary to correct them.

- Give them some sentences in English which illustrate a particular grammar point. Some of the sentences should, however, contain mistakes. The students use a grammar book or a grammar summary in their coursebook to check the sentences. For example, ask the students to refer to a summary of the form of the present simple to check the following sentences.

  My father work in a bank.
  Does you go to school by bus?
  My brother don't like school.
  I like English.
  My mother drive a red car.
  My best friend doesn't goes to my school.

- For revision of various grammar points, give groups of students one grammar point each to look up. They then prepare a poster presentation for the other groups.

- Dictionary race: give the students a list of words in either English or L1. They have to look them up in a dictionary to find the translation.

Which of the above ideas have you already used? If you haven't used any, plan the introduction of some resource work in your class and try some of the activities. If you already use some of them, try out a new one.

4 English outside class

Good language learners use opportunities outside the classroom to improve their English. Raise your students' awareness of things they can do to help themselves to learn outside the classroom. Ask them (in groups) to BRAINSTORM a list of things they can do outside the class to help themselves to learn. Give them some examples first. They should try to come up with a list of ten things.

Here are some ideas.

- Write to a penfriend in English.
- Listen to English pop songs and learn a verse or the chorus.
- Get a graded reader from the library and read it.
- Stick labels with the English words on them on things in your bedroom (e.g. *wardrobe*, *mirror*).
- Spend ten minutes every day looking at your English book.
- Go up to tourists and ask them some questions.
- Memorise a short dialogue from your coursebook.
- Test yourself on vocabulary learnt in class.
- Watch programmes in English on TV (if they are not all dubbed).
- Write down all the English words you see in the street (shop names, adverts, etc.).
- Think of five English questions to ask your teacher.
- Do an exercise from your workbook every day and check your answers in the key.

The groups compare their lists and decide on the ten best ideas. Each student then chooses one to do for that week, and has to report back the following week on what he/she did and how successful it was.

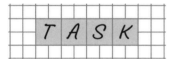

Which of the ideas above would you encourage weaker students to choose? Why?

5 Error awareness

Good language learners learn from their mistakes. You can help to raise students' awareness of error and this can help weaker learners once again.

Error spotting

Choose a text, or part of one, from the students' coursebook, perhaps one they have already read. Rewrite it with mistakes in it: these could be mistakes of spelling, aspects of grammar, vocabulary, organisation and so on. You could use a range of types of mistake or just one type. Give it to the students, give them a time limit to spot the mistakes. (You could make this into a graded task by adapting it for different levels, as in Chapter 5.) They check in pairs or groups to find the original text in their coursebook and check if they found all the mistakes.

Error checklists

Collect common errors and write them onto a poster, along with their correct version. This should be displayed in the classroom for students to refer to. Students can also keep their own 'personal error' sheets in their file: they should record errors they have made, particularly common errors, with their correct versions and refer to this before handing in a piece of written work.

6 The good language learner

Ask the students to brainstorm a list of things that the good language learner does and a list of things that the bad language learner does. Give each character a name, e.g. Fluent Florence and Terrible Terence.

Fluent Florence:
… always speaks English in class.
… learns from her mistakes.
… listens when the teacher is talking.
… reads her English book on the bus …

Terrible Terence:
… daydreams in his English class.
… speaks his own language in class.
… never listens to the teacher.
… often loses his notebook …

Use this as a reminder to the students of good and bad learning strategies and behaviour throughout the year. Don't let them glorify Terrible Terence!

7 Strategies for skills work

As an extension of the above, you can help raise students' awareness of good and bad learning strategies when it comes to the different skills: speaking, listening, reading and writing. This can be done through quizzes, discussion or reading or listening activities, e.g. you could do a simple quiz (in English or L1) to raise students' awareness of how to approach reading. Write some questions like the examples below and give them to the students.

> *Which of the following are a good idea when you read English?*
> *a) look up every word you don't know*
> *b) guess the meaning of new words*
> *c) try to understand the general topic …*

Discuss the answers in L1 afterwards.

◆ SEE PHOTOCOPIABLE PAGES 7 AND 8 FOR MORE IDEAS

8 Keeping records of work

It is important that students know what they are supposed to have learned and that they have a clear idea of their strengths and weaknesses as language learners. This is an important part of making learners feel responsible for their own learning, and encouraging them to try to improve.

End-of-lesson summaries can be used for students to think about what they have learned in a particular lesson, and they are very useful when students come to revise. Use a simple format so that students can complete them at the end of every lesson, e.g.

> *Date:*
>
> *What we learned today:*
>
> *What I found easy:*
>
> *What I found difficult:*
>
> *Homework task:*

When you first introduce these, you can give a little time at the end of each class to filling them in. When the students have got used to doing it, they can do it alone after the class. You will need to check from time to time that they have been doing it.

Summaries can also be used at the end of a topic-based unit of work or project, e.g.

> *This unit of work was about:*
>
> *We studied the following language points:*
>
> *We practised the following skills:*
>
> *What I did well:*
>
> *What I did not do well:*
>
> *What I am going to do to improve:*

Summaries can also be used to look at a block of work over a few weeks. The students can look back at their end-of-lesson summaries and fill in a more complete form. ◆ SEE PHOTOCOPIABLE PAGE 9
This is particularly useful in preparation for an individual counselling session (SEE CHAPTER 11, PAGE 73), a self-access lesson (SEE CHAPTER 7) or prior to a test.

It is important that you look at the students' records because it may be that they are over- or underestimating their level and their progress. It is a good idea to spend some time speaking to students individually about what they have put. If this is not always possible, monitor as they do the task and speak to those who you think are not evaluating themselves accurately, or collect the summaries in and then see who you need to speak to.

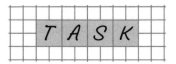

Does your coursebook contain useful learner training activities? Make a list of them.

Look back at the ideas suggested in this unit. Are there any areas that your coursebook does not cover? Decide on some activities to supplement your coursebook.

PART B **Coping**

CHAPTER 5

Grading tasks

The idea here is that students work on the same basic activity but with different tasks graded at varying levels of difficulty.

1 An example – dictation

Select a text to dictate to the students but give different students a different task to do:

- Give the students in the strongest group (e.g. blue group) a blank piece of paper.
- Give the middle-level group (e.g. green group) a gapped version of the text to be dictated.
- Give the lowest-level group (e.g. yellow group) a complete version of the text to be dictated with multiple-choice options for some of the words or expressions.
- Dictate the text in the normal way, reading it through once at normal speed and then dictating it in chunks, pausing to allow the students to complete their tasks. The students in the strongest group write down everything. Those in the middle-level group fill in the gaps in their text and those in the lowest-level group choose the correct word or expression from the choices given.
- After reading it out in chunks, read the whole text out again at normal speed for students to check their work individually.
- As an optional task you can get the students who did the same task to check their work with each other (i.e. blue with blue, green with green, yellow with yellow).
- Then regroup the students into multicoloured groups, i.e. groups of one yellow, one blue, one green student. The students then check their work together. They should not show each other their texts but talk through them, checking that everything is there and words are correctly spelt as they go. You should monitor and help as necessary.
- A whole-class feedback should not actually be necessary but you could, as a final stage, give students a copy of the original text to compare with or refer students to their coursebook if the text came from there.

(I first came across this idea in *Models and Metaphors in Language Teacher Training*, Tessa Woodward, CUP, 1991.)

Here is an example of a text.

> *Friday 13th November*
>
> *What a day. My alarm clock didn´t ring so I overslept. I woke up at ten o´clock with a terrible toothache. I suddenly remembered I had an appointment with the dentist at quarter past ten. I ran out of the house and down the street. Then I saw some girls laughing at me. I looked down. I was still in my pyjama trousers. I was very embarrassed. I ran back home but then I found I didn´t have my keys. I couldn´t open the door. I got a ladder from the garage and started to climb up to my bedroom window. But the ladder was very old and it broke. I fell off and broke my leg. Now I´m in hospital. My tooth still hurts and my leg hurts, too!*

SEE PHOTOCOPIABLE PAGE 10 for the gapped version and the multiple-choice version.

2 Advantages and disadvantages of using graded tasks

What are the advantages?

- All students are challenged at an appropriate level of difficulty and can get involved in doing the task. No one should be left behind or have nothing to do.
- All students can succeed in completing the task given to them, and this is motivating for them.
- You can design different tasks for lots of different activity types (e.g. listening, reading, vocabulary practice).
- The multicoloured checking stage empowers the weaker students since they are the ones who are most likely to have a complete and correct version of the text. They are therefore in a position to help the stronger students.
- This checking stage also promotes student co-operation and tolerance.

T A S K

Cover the disadvantages below. What are the disadvantages of using graded tasks? Can you think of any solutions to these disadvantages?

What are the disadvantages?

- There is much more preparation for the teacher.
- Students may feel labelled as weak, medium or strong and therefore embarrassed. The weaker students in particular may feel demotivated.
- Stronger students may resent always having to work 'harder' (as they see it).
- The teacher may get confused about who is doing what, especially in a large class.

What are the solutions?

- It does mean more preparation, but the tasks can be kept and hopefully used again with other classes and by other teachers. It is worth building up a bank of this kind of task and keeping them for future use, perhaps with a group of teachers, maybe even from different schools.
- Let the students choose which 'colour' activity they want. When you introduce the system of graded activities, make it lighthearted, e.g. *Who's feeling tired today? OK, you can do a yellow activity.* Colours are better than numbers or letters since they don't have grading associations. (You could use other names, e.g. animals, fruit). You should keep a note of what level of

activity each student chooses each time for evaluation purposes. If you use the same coding system, the students will get to know which activity is most likely to suit them. Occasionally you may want to intervene if you feel they are over- or underchallenging themselves.

- If the students have a choice, they can perhaps sometimes be allowed to do an easier task. But it is up to you to ensure they do challenge themselves sufficiently. Individual counselling may help if necessary.
- Good classroom management and organisational skills are crucial here. The following steps may help:

When preparing the worksheets, write in one corner the colour, or actually mark each one with a coloured pen/crayon after you've copied them.
When asking what colour activity the students want to do, get them to put their hands up and count them to ensure the groups are roughly equally sized.
Before doing the activity, it may be useful to group the students according to colour so they can't see the other groups' worksheets.
When regrouping the students into multicoloured groups for checking, the students will have to move. Give clear instructions for them to go round saying their colour to each other, to find the appropriate partners. They should sit down as soon as they have found their group of three. You can then add any extra students to the groups if numbers make it necessary.

Look at the text below, or use a text from your coursebook. Devise a gapped text and a multiple-choice text for use with it.

A bug is an insect. So why are mistakes in computer programmes called bugs? It is because the first computer bug was in fact a real insect. The first computers were very, very big and filled a whole room. A computer called Mark 1 broke down one day so technicians looked inside it. They found a dead moth. The programmer started to call computer errors `bugs´ and the name stuck.

---

3 Picture dictation

This is a fun activity and can be adapted to provide practice in many different lexical and structural areas. This example practises describing people, their appearance and clothes. The stronger students start with a piece of paper and have to draw the people from scratch. The middle-level students are given outlines of the people, and the weaker ones the outlines with some details filled in.

Read out the text below to the students. The stronger students have to listen and understand everything in order to complete the task, whereas the middle level and weaker students with the partly drawn pictures do not have to understand everything.

SEE PHOTOCOPIABLE PAGE 11

This is a picture of my grandfather and grandmother. They are quite strange! My grandfather is very tall and thin. He´s bald but he´s got thick black eyebrows and a big thick moustache. He wears glasses on the end of his big nose. He´s got small bright eyes and he stares hard at you. He always looks very serious; he never smiles. He looks quite frightening if you don´t know him, I think. He usually wears an old jacket and trousers which are too long. He uses a walking stick because he can´t walk very well. Oh and he´s always smoking his pipe of course.

My grandmother, on the other hand, is very short and fat, almost round. She has short curly hair. She wears glasses on the end of her nose too. She's very different from my grandfather; she's always smiling and happy. She usually wears a blouse with a high neck and a long skirt. She loves reading so she's always got a book in her hand. Oh, and she always wears a big gold heart on a chain round her neck: it was the first present she got from my grandfather.

4 Vocabulary activities

Crazy texts

Read the following text. What do you notice about it?

The day a policeman saw a man walking along the street down a penguin. He went up to the have and said, 'Excuse me, sir. Is that big penguin?'
'No,' replied the man,' It isn't mine. I just found street.'
'Well, why don't that take it to the zoo?'
'That's a red idea,' said the cat. 'I will.'
The next day, the policeman saw the man bad. He zoo very surprised because the penguin was still with talk.
'Excuse it, sir,' said the park, 'but didn't you take the penguin to out zoo yesterday?'
'Oh yes, I are,' replied the man, 'and we really enjoyed it. Today we're going to saw to the cinema.'

This is an example of a crazy text: there are a number of words in it that are wrong. The most difficult task you can give the students to do with this is to find the wrong words and replace them with the correct ones. This task would be suitable for the strongest students.

Cover the ideas below. How could you adjust the task to varying degrees to make it easier? Think of as many ways as you can before reading on.

Here are some ways of adjusting the level of difficulty of the task:
- Tell the students how many wrong words there are before they begin. They have to identify them and correct them.
- Indicate which lines the wrong words are in (and the number of words in each line). Students identify and correct them.
- Before students go on to correct the wrong words, they receive feedback on whether they have correctly identified them (e.g. via an answer sheet).
- Underline the wrong words before you copy the text. Students correct them.
- Give students a jumbled list of the correct words to replace the wrong ones.

Here is the correct version of the text. The words in capitals are the ones that were wrong in the crazy text:

ONE day a policeman saw a man walking along the street WITH a penguin. He went up to the MAN and said, 'Excuse me, sir. Is that YOUR penguin?'
'No,' replied the man.'It isn't mine. I just found IT.'
'Well, why don't YOU take it to the zoo?'
'That's a GOOD idea,' said the MAN. 'I will.'

The next day, the policeman saw the man AGAIN. He WAS very surprised because the penguin was still with HIM.
'Excuse ME, sir,' said the POLICEMAN, 'but didn't you take the penguin to THE zoo yesterday?'
'Oh yes, I DID,' replied the man, 'and we really enjoyed it. Today we're going to GO to the cinema.'

Wordsearch

There are ways of making this more or less difficult. Look at this example.

Find the following words in the square (→ and ↓):

bed	bookshelf	mirror	television	carpet	lamp
sofa	cupboard	fridge	wardrobe	armchair	cooker
table	CD player				

S	O	F	A	C	F	E	P	T	A
C	W	A	R	D	R	O	B	E	P
U	C	B	M	P	I	T	O	L	M
P	O	E	C	L	D	A	O	E	I
B	O	D	H	A	G	B	K	V	R
O	K	M	A	Y	E	L	S	I	R
A	E	Y	I	E	N	E	H	S	O
R	R	U	R	R	G	L	E	I	R
D	L	A	M	P	B	I	L	O	F
C	A	R	P	E	T	K	F	N	E

This is a very easy task and only requires the students to recognise the words in the square.

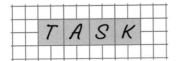

Cover the list below. How could you adapt this task to make it more difficult? See how many ideas you can think of for making it progressively more challenging. Then compare your ideas with those below.

Ideas to make the task more challenging:
Give students skeleton versions of the words, e.g. s __ __ a, m __ __ r __ r.
Give them the L1 equivalents of the words.
Give them pictures of the words.
Tell them there are 14 things in the word square that they can find in the house.
Tell them to find as many 'things in the house' as they can.
Tell them to find as many words connected to one topic as they can and to identify the topic.

As a follow-up, you should check that students know the meaning of the words. You could supply the definitions or a translation which the students have to match to the words. Or you could get the fast finishers to produce these definitions.

5 Reading and listening

Students can also be given different tasks for listening and reading comprehension activities. Look at this text and task.

(From *Freeform 2*, page 35; Downie, Gray, Jiménez, Richmond English, 1993.)

The task requires the students to absorb information from both texts and identify how many differences there are between the two, and what the differences are. This can be made easier for weaker students if you give them a grid (empty or partly completed) indicating the type of information they are looking for, e.g.

	Advertisement	Article
Concert days and dates		Thursday 22nd Nov Friday 23rd Nov Monday 26th Nov
Location: 22nd 23rd 25th 26th 29th 30th	Aberdeen Exhibition and Conference Centre	
Prices of tickets		Aberdeen £14 Wembley £15

Now look at this listening text. Can you devise graded tasks for it?

Listening: prices

Tapescript

Well, on our show tonight we are looking at personal stereos for under £50.00. First there's the Boots PSX20. Now this is really excellent value for just £7.99. It looks wonderful ... bright pink and green. Then we have the Philips Moving Sound AQ6404. A nice personal stereo this, at £27.99, though we didn't like the colour much. We also looked at two personal stereos from Sanyo – the MGP310D at £29.99 and the MGR78 which costs £27.99. The more expensive model has a better sound, but neither of these is great value. Then of course there's the Sony Walkman and here you really are paying for the name – £49.99. Expensive! But the best value of all the machines we tested was the Panasonic RQ535V. A really great machine and excellent value at £34.99.

(From *Freeform 2*, Unit 5, Assignment 3, page 27)

Possible graded activities:

For stronger students, get them to do a very intensive listening task by completing the following grid:

	Model	Price	Colour	Opinion
1				
2				

Middle-level students can fill in a partially completed grid, as shown in the previous activity.

Weaker students could be given a grid already completed but with some wrong information that they have to correct. If you limit the wrong information to the model numbers and prices this will make it easier still, e.g.

Model	Price	Colour	Opinion
Boots PSX20	£8.99	pink & green	excellent value looks wonderful
Philips Moving Sound AQ6499	£27.99	don't know	nice, but didn't like the colour
Sanyo MGP310D	£39.99	don't know	better sound than other not good value

1 Look at your coursebook and select some material that you want to use soon with your mixed-ability class.

2 Decide if each task as given in the book is most suitable for the weaker, middle or stronger students in your class.

3 Decide how you could adapt each of the tasks to make them easier or more difficult for the other students in your class.

CHAPTER 6

Self access

Another possibility for coping with mixed-ability classes is different students working on different tasks, with different resources in the classroom, individually or in groups. In this chapter, we will consider aspects of the self-access approach.

1 Advantages of this approach

It caters for a wide mix of ability.

Teaching can be tailored to the individual's needs.

Learners work on something that they think is useful and interesting.

It increases learner autonomy, and gives students a sense of responsibility for their own learning.

You can spend more time with those students who need your help.

It adds variety to your classes.

2 Materials that can be used

It can be time consuming to build up a bank of materials for students to use, but well worth it. There are many types of material suitable for self access and you don't need to create a lot of materials from scratch as many can be found ready made. If you do want to create materials (e.g. sets of questions for games), one idea to reduce your work is to get a class of higher-level students in the school to make up the questions for the lower levels. This also has the advantage of involving the students from the outset in the self-access centre.

Students' workbooks

Provide a list of exercises that students haven't done, with a key in order to check their own work. If their workbooks do not contain one, you will need to copy the one from the teacher's book or provide one.

Books of grammar and vocabulary exercises

If these are not photocopiable, cut up a copy of the book and laminate each sheet to ensure it is kept clean and in good condition. The students can write their answers to the exercises in their notebooks, then check with the key.

Readers and accompanying tapes

Graded readers can be provided at different levels of difficulty. Provide headphones for listening to the tapes if possible, if not a tape recorder for a group in the corner of the room will do.

Video

If you have a video recorder, you can make video cassettes available, preferably with accompanying worksheets. If you are using published EFL video material, these will be available in book form. If you are using authentic off-air recordings (bearing in mind copyright restrictions), you may need to make up worksheets. Rather than creating a new worksheet for each, create one that can be used for many different programmes, such as the example on PHOTOCOPIABLE PAGE 12.

Computers and CD-ROM

These are ideal for self-access work as immediate feedback is provided and the technology is motivating for teenagers.

Audio cassettes

Copies of supplementary resource books of listening material, with the tape, can be used, as can authentic material such as pop songs, along with worksheets and copies of the lyrics. Ask the students themselves to provide the songs and lyrics.

Magazines

Subscribe to magazines produced for learners of English, e.g. *BBC English*, or, try to get hold of some produced for English teenagers. As with authentic video recordings, provide re-useable worksheets with general questions to answer about the contents and then a more in-depth vocabulary and summarising task for one article of their choice.

Games

Board games based on questions in English, e.g. Trivial Pursuit, Snakes and Ladders (SEE PAGE 48) or word games, e.g. Scrabble, Boggle, are another possibility for self access. Dominoes sets can be made for many language areas, e.g. matching words and pictures, opposites or L1 and English words, e.g.

Reference books

Bilingual and monolingual dictionaries, grammar books and encyclopaedias, should be available for students to refer to.

3 Organisation of the materials

Ideally, every school would have a permanent self-access room with computers, CD-ROM, video, listening facilities, readers and accompanying tapes, worksheets, grammar exercises with accompanying key, games and so on. Most schools do not have the space for this, however, and the self-access facilities may be more limited.

It is still possible to have a small but perfectly adequate self-access centre contained in a cupboard. If you don't have a cupboard, even a self-access box can be sufficient!

It is very important that materials are indexed and clearly organised:

- Laminated worksheets can be kept in files clearly marked as 'grammar', 'listening' or 'vocabulary'. Answer keys should be provided.

- If copyright and your school budget permit photocopies, these can be kept in plastic envelopes in the file. These will need replacing now and again so you will need to check on a regular basis how many are left.

- It is useful to use a system to indicate levels of difficulty. This could be done with colours, e.g. blue for most difficult, green for medium, yellow for the easiest (preferably the same colour system you use in class for graded tasks).

- If you are using the self-access collection with different years, you will need also to mark which year the materials are designed for.

- Readers should be arranged according to levels of difficulty (use the same colour coding that you use for other materials) and also, if you have quite a large collection, in order according to type (e.g. classics, non-fiction, crime). You could supply a photocopiable index of the readers for easy reference. It is useful for students to borrow the graded readers and take them home, too. Provide a notebook in which they write their name, the title of the book, the date they borrowed it and the date they returned it.
- An index of video and one for audio materials with brief summaries of the contents will help students choose what they want to work with. Have a space on the summary form for students to write a brief 'review'.

As well as organising the materials so that students can find their way around them, it is also important to train students to put them back in the right place. If you have board games, put a label on the lid saying what the box should contain (e.g. two dice, a board, six counters) so that students can easily check everything is there when they begin and when they finish. Laminated worksheets should be clearly numbered so they can be put back in the right place in the file.

4 Student choice in what they do

It is important that students choose something that is useful for them in terms of improving their English. It is also important that they choose something that they like doing to ensure that their motivation is kept up. If there is a mismatch between their needs and their likes, then a compromise may be reached in which they spend part of the time on something they need and the rest on something they like.

You will need to set aside some time to introduce the students to the self-access materials when you first use them. You could provide a worksheet in L1 with questions that the students have to answer, e.g. *Where are the video cassettes? How do you choose a video? Where can you find a worksheet?*

This should be done the lesson before you actually want to use the self-access materials. Make sure the students understand why you are using them as well as the different possibilities available. Get them to choose what they want to do in advance so that they can start work immediately in the self-access lesson.

Provide a form for them to complete in which they have to write down what they plan to do and why, like the one on PHOTOCOPIABLE PAGE 13.

Here is a partially completed example:

Date	What I plan to do in self access	Why	What I did in self access (and time spent)	Student comment	Teacher comment
20/10	Listening Unit 4 Ex 3 in coursebook	Listening we did in class was difficult for me	Listening Unit 4 Ex 3 (15 mins)	Listening was easier - I need to do more.	Keep up the listening practice - try a video next time?
			Vocabulary ex on professions (1. 3) (10 mins)	I got the vocab ex right.	Well done with the vocabulary.
4/11	Video number 5	More listening practice	Video number 5 (20 mins)	It was fun but it was easy.	Let me help you choose a video next time.
			Started playing Scrabble.		

Students hand this in to you so you can check that they are choosing sensibly. If they are not doing something appropriate, then use gentle persuasion to encourage them to choose more suitable activities.

5 Ensure students are working

The teacher's main roles in self-access lessons or parts of lessons are as:

Provider – the teacher provides the materials.

Guide – the teacher may need to help the students choose and find appropriate materials.

Monitor – the teacher needs to ensure all the students are working and using English and may need to intervene to help or correct .

Resource – the teacher should be available to answer any questions that students may have about the material they are working on, or be able to direct students to another reference source if necessary.

Instructions on any materials for self access need to be very clear. You shouldn't have to give instructions orally, but you will need to check as you go around the class that all the students have understood and are following the written instructions.

Some activities may be done individually, others in groups or pairs. The teacher may need to help organise groupings. If discipline problems arise, the teacher may need to intervene and change groupings.

Self access obviously means that the students are taking on greater responsibility for their own learning. Lazy or tired students may see it as an opportunity to take a rest. Disruptive students may take the opportunity to play around while your back is turned. How can you avoid this?

- By introducing self access gradually: explain why you are doing it and start doing it occasionally and for short periods of time.
- By making sure everybody has chosen something appropriate to work on.
- By checking that everyone understands what they are supposed to do (check the weaker students first).
- By making sure everybody has something to do all the time (make sure students know what to do when they finish an activity, i.e. evaluate it, replace it in the file and choose something else).
- By closer monitoring of the weaker and more difficult students.
- By getting the students to keep a record of each activity they do and how long they spend on it, to evaluate it and say what they learned from it.
- By having a clear disciplinary procedure which all the students are aware of.

6 Monitoring students' progress

The record sheets that the students complete are very important. You can fill in comments too if you think it is useful. Using these with self evaluation and individual counselling, you can see if the student is making progress.

If you do not have self-access materials already available, make a list of materials that you could collect together and use. Discuss with your colleagues how the materials could best be organised and used. Plan a schedule for getting the materials together. If you already have self-access materials, could you now add to them in any way?

CHAPTER 7

Content teaching

One of the differences among learners is in their knowledge of the world, their talents and interests, general knowledge and knowledge of other school subjects. Just because a learner has not been a successful language learner does not mean that he/she is lacking in knowledge or skills in other areas. By providing opportunities in the English class for students to make use of this other knowledge we can do the following.

- Encourage a sense of self esteem.
- Encourage respect and create bonds between learners of different levels.
- Ensure everyone has something to contribute.
- Motivate weaker students to contribute and take an interest.
- Increase the value of English as a genuine means of communication.
- Provide opportunities for acquisition of the language.
- Give English lessons an educational purpose beyond the teaching of language.
- Make lessons relevant to the learners by catering for their interests.
- Take learners' minds off the fact that they are learning language forms and enable them to focus on meaning and communication.
- Allow learners to show off their knowledge and 'teach the teacher'.

For these kinds of activities it is best to have students working in groups of mixed language level.

1 Quizzes

These can take various forms and are very motivating for students. Try a quiz on a particular subject area, e.g. geography or have a variety of subjects. It is best if you liaise with the relevant teacher(s) to find out what the students have been studying, then make up questions accordingly.

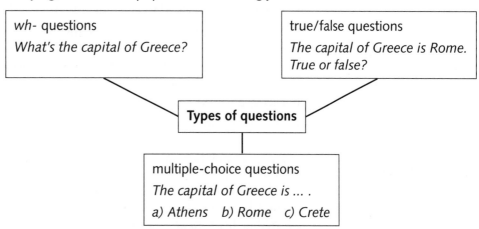

Give each group of students a list of the questions and a time limit to work on answering them. Give each group a team name and ask them to tell you their answers for each question. They score a point for each correct answer. The winner is the team with most points at the end. (Don't correct pronunciation or grammatical errors during the activity as this will detract from the purpose; you may decide, however, to make a note of any errors and do a correction spot at the end of the lesson or in the next lesson.)

Quizzes can also be done orally. You can do this in different ways.

- Each team has a question to answer in turn. If they can't answer it, it is passed on to the other teams in turn, who can win a bonus point by answering correctly. You could let students choose the subject category.

- Questions are asked and whichever team thinks they know the answer can have a go at answering by making a predetermined noise (e.g. saying *Ping!* or *Beep!*) and saying their answer. If they are right, they score a point; if they are wrong, another team can have a go.

- Teams can also make up their own questions. Monitor to help with and check the language as they write their questions. During the quiz itself, try not to interrupt to correct the language but leave it until afterwards. Only intervene if communication problems occur and don't make a big issue of it.

You can also design quizzes to practise specific language points, e.g.

... dates (history): *When did a person first walk on the moon?* (1969)
... past passives (science, history): *Where was John Lennon shot?* (New York)
... past simple (history): *When did Franco die?* (1975)
... present passive (general knowledge, science): *What is water made of?* (hydrogen and oxygen)

You can also use quizzes for *How ...?* questions, e.g.

1 How old are the Alps?   a) 400 million years   b) 50 million years
   c) 15 million years   (Answer: c)

2 How fast can an ostrich run?   a) 50 km per hour   b) 60 km per hour
   c) 70 km per hour   (Answer: a)

TASK

Devise a short general knowledge quiz to practise a specific language point that you will be introducing or practising with your class soon.

2 Games

Noughts and crosses

- Draw a noughts and crosses square on the board as illustrated on the left.

- Prepare questions in advance; you will need to have several ready for each square. Again, they could be on one subject, such as geography, or practising one structure, or they could be a mixture. They should be numbered to correspond with a particular square.

- Divide the class into two teams: noughts and crosses.

- They take it in turns to choose a square, then you ask them a question.

- If they answer correctly, you mark it with their sign (O or X). If they don't, it remains available. The next time someone chooses it, ask a different question.

- The aim is to get a line of three noughts or crosses in any direction.

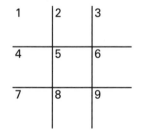
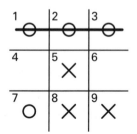

Obviously, with a large class, the size of the two groups may be very large. It is a good idea, then, to get the students working in smaller groups after you have played the game a couple of times, with a student playing the role of question master. You could supply the questions (the same ones for the different groups) or get the groups to make up questions to pass on to another group.

Pictionary

This is a commercial game, but it can easily be played in class. The game can initially be played with the class divided into two teams, but is again best done in smaller groups. The teams can take it in turns to play.

- Give one student a word, expression or sentence on a piece of paper. The student has to come out to the board and try to draw it.

- The rest of the team tries to guess what was written on the piece of paper. These can be words, expressions or short sentences, depending on the level of the class, e.g.

Words	Expressions	Short sentences
rose	*an elephant's trunk*	*The Eiffel Tower is in Paris.*
television	*a dog barking*	*Spiders have eight legs.*
bread	*a hot sunny day*	*The phone's ringing.*

- The language you use here should be known but you could supply a translation on the piece of paper which weaker students can look at before they draw.

- The other members of the team have to guess in English. If they don't get it within the time limit you set, the other team can have one guess.

This game will allow students who are good at drawing well (and quickly) to shine.

What P ...?

Again, do this with the whole class in two (named) teams before dividing the class into smaller groups.

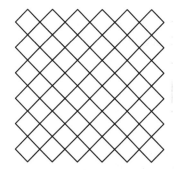

- Copy the grid on the left onto the board, or preferably onto an overhead transparency. In each diamond write a letter, or pair of letters. You need to prepare questions in advance.

- Each team takes it in turns to choose a diamond; you ask them a question.

- If they answer correctly, they win that diamond, i.e. you write the team name in it.

- They start on the left-hand side of the grid, and the aim is to make a line across the grid. When they reach the other side they have won.

- They cannot ask for a diamond that has already been occupied by the other team. Each diamond they ask for must join onto the side of one they have already won.

  Questions are of this type:

  What P is the capital of France?
  Who was the JL who was shot dead in New York in 1980?
  What H is produced by bees?
  What W is made of hydrogen and oxygen?

- You could choose a particular theme for all the questions or have a mix of subject areas.

- After playing with the whole class, you can divide the students into four or six teams; supply each pair of teams with a grid (if it's laminated it could be used again and again). Give a set of questions to each team.

(This game is based on a TV game show called *Blockbusters*.)

Three, two, one

This works well with the whole class divided into four or more teams.

● Read out each description and when a team thinks they know what is being described they can volunteer an answer.

● If they answer correctly at the beginning of the description, they score three points, in the middle two points and at the end, one point.

● If their guess is wrong, they cannot try again immediately, but must wait until another team has tried to answer.

Questions are of this type:

This is about an animal. When this animal is born it is only about two centimetres long, blind and helpless. It crawls up its mother's stomach and into her pouch and it stays there for about six months. The baby is called a joey. This animal grows to a height of about two metres and moves by hopping on its back legs. It lives in one continent only, Australia. What is the name of this animal? (Answer: a kangaroo.)

This game provides excellent listening practice for students.

(The idea for this activity comes from a book called *Who Knows?*, Neville Britten, Addison-Wesley Longman, 1990)

Snakes and ladders

This is another game that can be played in small groups. You need to supply sets of questions on cards along with each board. Players take it in turns to throw the dice and move their counters on from the 'Start' box. Another member of the team picks up a question card and asks the question. If they answer the question correctly, they go forward three squares; if they get it wrong, they go back three squares. If they land at the bottom of a ladder they go up; if they land on a snake's mouth they go down the snake. The winner is the person to make it 'home' (the 'Finish' box) first.

◆ SEE PHOTOCOPIABLE PAGE 14

Decide on an appropriate time to play a quiz game with the students. Decide whether you want to use general questions or concentrate on specific subject areas. Prepare one of the above games. Try to encourage a colleague to make a different one so that you can then swap.

3 Maths tricks

Practising numbers and mathematics in English can be very motivating and allows the students who have a skill in this area to use it. Here are some number tricks to do with the students. They are best read out to them. You may find that they know of others which you can get them to do in English.

Trick 1

Give all the students the following instructions:

Think of a number. Multiply the number by three. Add one. Multiply by three again. Add the number you originally thought of.

Now ask for their answers. From their answers you can tell them what their original number was: if the answer is a two-digit number, e.g. 21, 43, the answer is the first digit, i.e. 2, 4. If it is a three-digit number, the answer is the first two digits and so on.

Example:

Original number:	12
Multiply by 3:	$12 \times 3 = 36$
Add 1:	$36 + 1 = 37$
Multiply by 3 again:	$37 \times 3 = 111$
Add the original number:	$111 + 12 = 123$

The original number must be 12.

Trick 2

Give all the students the following instructions:

Think of a number. Double it. Add four. Multiply by five. Add twelve. Multiply by ten.

Ask for their total. Subtract 320 and remove the two 0s – this gives you the number they originally thought of.

Example:

Original number: 7

Double it:	$7 \times 2 = 14$
Add 4:	$14 + 4 = 18$
Multiply by 5:	$18 \times 5 = 90$
Add 12:	$90 + 12 = 102$
Multiply by 10:	$102 \times 10 = 1020$
Subtract 320:	$1020 - 320 = 700$
Remove the 0s:	7 is the answer.

4 Number puzzles

There are also number puzzles. The important thing here is that students have to explain to the class or write down in English how they reached their answer, even if much of their group discussion is in L1.

Puzzle 1

A dealer bought a painting for £7,000 and sold it for £8,000. He then bought it back again for £9,000 and then sold it again for £10,000. How much profit did he make?

Answer: £2,000. (He spent £16,000 in total and received £18,000. His profit was the difference: £2,000.)

Puzzle 2

Complete the box with the correct number. (Clue: look at the numbers above, above to the left and on the left of each number.)

1	1	1	1
1	3	5	7
1	5	13	25
1	7	25	?

Answer: 63 (Each number is the sum of the numbers above, above to the left and to the left of it, so the missing number is the sum of 25, 13 and 25.)

Puzzle 3

A man ate 100 bunches of grapes in five days. Each day he ate six bunches more than the day before. How many bunches of grapes did he eat on the first day?

Answer: 8 (This is one way to work it out. On day two he ate $x + 6$ bunches, on day three, $x + 12$ bunches, on day four, $x + 18$ bunches and on day five, $x + 24$ bunches. If you add $6 + 12 + 18 + 24$ you get 60. That leaves 40 bunches, divided by five days, which makes 8. Thus on the first day he ate 8 bunches, on the second day 14, on the third day 20 and so on.)

Puzzle 4

A man has seven pedigree animals. Some are cats and some are dogs. Each dog eats five biscuits and each cat eats four. Thirty two biscuits are eaten. How many dogs and how many cats are there?

Answer: Four dogs and three cats (If each animal eats four biscuits, that comes to 28 biscuits, so there are four left over – one for each dog.)

5 Logic puzzles

As with the number puzzles, it is important that students give their explanations to these in English. Here, again, you will find that the students who are good at working out these puzzles are not necessarily those who are good at English.

The students can work in groups on the solution. You can introduce an element of competition here by saying the first group to solve the problem and explain it in English is the winner.

The students may need access to bilingual dictionaries or they can ask you how to say things they are unsure of. Once again, this enables students to focus on using all the language they **can** use rather than practise specific structures.

Puzzle 1

Alexander, Paul and Peter are a forward, a defence and a goalkeeper in a football team. The goalkeeper is the shortest of the three and he is single. Alexander is Paul's wife's brother and he is taller than the person who defends him. Who plays in which position?

Answer: Peter must be the goalkeeper (he's the shortest and he isn't married). Alexander must be the forward (he's taller than the person who defends him). Paul must be the defence.

Puzzle 2

After a bank robbery, a policeman interviewed four witnesses who saw the robber escape: a taxi driver, a bus driver, a lady at the bus stop and a shopkeeper. The taxi driver said the robber was short and blond, wore glasses and was wearing a blue shirt. The bus driver said he had black hair, and was of medium height, wore glasses and was wearing a blue shirt. The lady at the bus stop said he was tall with red hair and glasses and was wearing a white shirt. The shopkeeper said he was short and bald with a blue shirt and he wasn't wearing glasses.

The policeman knew that only one detail from each witness's description was correct and that only one person correctly described that detail. What did the bank robber look like?

Answer:

	Taxi driver	Bus driver	Lady at bus stop	Shopkeeper
height	short	medium	tall	short
hair	blond	black	red	bald
glasses	yes	yes	yes	no
shirt	blue	blue	white	blue

Because only one detail from each person's description is correct, and only one person got that detail correct, this is the description of the bank robber:

He didn't wear glasses.
He had a white shirt.
He was of medium height.
He had blond hair.

Puzzle 3

A farmer is travelling to the market with his dog, a rabbit and a basket of carrots. He comes to a river and needs to cross it in a small boat. There is only room for him and one animal or the basket. He can't leave the dog alone with the rabbit because the dog will eat the rabbit, or the rabbit alone with the carrots because the rabbit will eat the carrots. How can they all get across the river?

Answer:

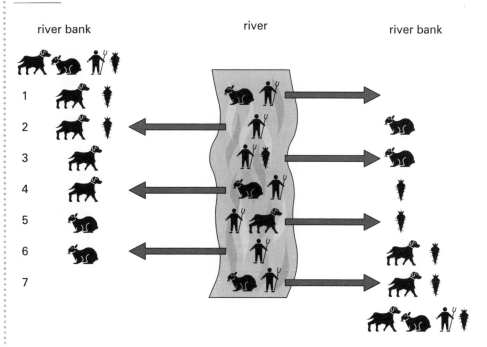

Puzzle 4

An explorer goes one kilometre to the south, turns and goes one kilometre to the east, turns again and goes one kilometre north. He arrives back where he started. Then he kills a bear. What colour is the bear?

Answer: White. It's a polar bear because he's at the North Pole.

6 Choosing topics

cookery

playing the guitar

listening to rock music

playing computer games

By letting students choose topics to work on you allow a very mixed group of students to satisfy a wide range of interests and thereby keep up interest and motivation.

My vocabulary

Vocabulary is very important and students should be encouraged to build up their knowledge of vocabulary as much as possible. While much of what the teacher presents at low levels is CORE VOCABULARY, the students can be encouraged to expand their personal vocabulary by exploring subjects that are interesting to them. This is motivating and something that students of all levels can do with the aid of a bilingual or picture dictionary.

- Ask the students to think of a topic in which they are interested or give them a list of possible topics, e.g. football, fashion, pop music, swimming, dogs.
- Ask them to draw a single image in simple outline (to fill a page) to represent their topic. See the examples on the left.
- The students can work in pairs or groups if they have chosen the same topics, or individually if they have a topic that no one else is interested in.
- Tell them to think of ten words associated with this topic in L1, then to find them, using a dictionary, in English. They should write them onto their drawing wherever they like, adding the L1 equivalent, a short sentence in English using the word or a small drawing to help them remember the meaning.
- This work could be presented as a poster or as a page in their vocabulary notebooks.
- When you have done this in class, students can do the same on a different topic of their choice for homework or in self-access slots.
- You should encourage weaker students to recycle core vocabulary in this way.
- With students who are not complete beginners, get them to give a short talk about their interest or hobby, using the vocabulary poster as a visual aid.

(This is based on an idea in *Vocabulary*, by John Morgan and Mario Rinvolucri, OUP, 1986.)

My lesson

This idea can be used as a warmer in your lessons. Ask the students to bring in a picture that is associated in some way with one of their interests or hobbies. Use this as the basis for BRAINSTORMING of vocabulary, perhaps about five words. In particular, encourage the weaker and less motivated students to bring in a picture; it will help them to feel involved in the classes when it is their picture that is the focus of attention.

Project work and student presentations

PROJECT WORK and STUDENT PRESENTATIONS offer an ideal opportunity for students to bring in their knowledge of the world and interests if they are allowed some choice in which topics to focus on. We will look at PROJECT WORK in more detail in Chapter 8 and student PRESENTATIONS in Chapter 9.

T A S K

Use PHOTOCOPIABLE PAGE 15, or something similar to find out about your students' strengths and interests. Then look at the coming work in your coursebook and decide on one idea from this chapter to include in your next unit of work.

Activities with different responses

Some classroom activities allow for different types of responses from different students. This is another very good option for mixed-ability classes since it allows students to do what they are good at and thereby raise self esteem. All of these activities involve the students in producing language (writing or speaking) at some point and all of them are based on groupwork. Groups should be organised so that students are mixed in terms of language level and other skills.

1 Project work

If students are working in groups on a project there will be different tasks to do. Let us imagine a project in which students are looking at the topic of food and health and are going to produce a poster and oral presentation as an end product.

Here are some of the different tasks which the students may need to carry out.

- Reading reference sources, finding out about food values and nutrition, revising notes from biology lessons.
- Thinking up a questionnaire about eating habits (in L1 if done outside class on family, friends, etc.; in English if it is to be done on classmates).
- Writing out or typing up the questionnaires.
- Carrying out the interviews in L1 or L2.
- Analysing questionnaires (statistics).
- Transferring statistical information to a graph or pie chart/bar chart.
- Finding or drawing pictures.
- Writing up descriptions and findings.
- Graphic display: designing and mounting the poster.
- Oral presentation of findings.

Different members of the group will be able to take on different responsibilities. The different tasks suggest the need for:

... reading skills (L1 or L2 depending on reference books)
... translation into L2
... using background knowledge about biology/chemistry
... knowledge of English vocabulary on the topic
... the ability to use a dictionary
... clear handwriting or typewriting or wordprocessing skills
... logical thinking/imagination for the questionnaire
... speaking skills
... knowledge of maths and statistics
... graphic skills
... artistic skills
... writing skills: text organisation, knowledge of grammar, punctuation, etc.

T A S K

Imagine another project in which students make a video of a 21st-century fashion show for their classmates. List the different tasks and skills that this might involve, then check your ideas with the suggestions on page 54.

Suggested tasks and skills

Tasks

designing the clothes
finding or making the clothes
modelling the clothes
helping the models dress/put on make-up
directing the fashion show and writing instructions for it
orally describing the clothes
writing a description of what each model is wearing
filming/videoing the fashion show
interviewing the designer(s)

Skills

the ability to draw
the ability to sew or make clothes from, e.g. paper, foil
knowledge of English vocabulary for describing clothes, materials, styles
language for describing ways of moving, direction, etc.
the ability to use a dictionary
clear handwriting or word processing skills
using a video camera
speaking skills
the ability to apply make-up

PHOTOCOPIABLE PAGE 16 provides students with a form which will help them to plan the steps of PROJECT WORK carefully and allocate tasks accordingly. It also includes sections for evaluation of the PROJECT WORK.

PROJECT WORK is therefore ideal for classes of mixed ability since there are many different tasks to be done, which demand different types and levels of skills. It is important that tasks are clearly allocated so that weaker, quieter or less enthusiastic students are actively involved.

2 Roleplays

Any speaking activity which involves students taking on different roles is suitable for mixed ability as the roles will vary in terms of the demands upon the speaker. That is, some of the roles may be bigger, some smaller, some more or less demanding in terms of language to be produced. Everyone can be involved but at their own level. ROLEPLAY is also a very versatile activity and can be used to practise a wide range of language items in many different situations.

Example:

A You have just ridden into B on your bicycle. You think it was his/her fault because he/she stepped into the road without looking. Get off your bike and go and speak to B.

B A stupid girl/boy on his/her bike (A) has just ridden into you. It was certainly A's fault and your leg is hurting badly. Go and speak to A.

C You are a policeman. You see two people arguing. They have just had an accident. You need to fill in a report.

> *Time of accident:*
> *Place:*
> *Names of parties involved:*
> *Reason for accident:*

Give the students time to prepare their roles first, by putting all the As, all the Bs and all the Cs together. Give the role of the policeman to the weaker students and help them more at the preparation stage by getting them to write down the questions they will need to ask. This preparation is not unnatural as they have a form to complete. The other roles require more creative and freer language use.

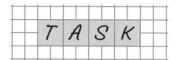

Choose one of the following situations and decide how roles could be designed to cater for mixed-ability groups:

interview with a pop group

two old friends who meet in a cafe by chance

a television programme or radio phone-in in which experts give advice to viewers or listeners on their problems.

3 Bilingual roleplays

In a bilingual ROLEPLAY there are three characters: one who speaks only English, one who speaks only L1, and one who speaks both languages. The situation and setting can be any, but the English-only speaker and the L1-only speaker want to communicate with each other and so must use the bilingual speaker as an interpreter. This is a very common real-life situation. With a mixed-ability class obviously the weaker students can take the part of the L1 speaker and stronger students the part of the English-only speaker. Here are some ideas.

Situation one (adapt to your teaching situation)

A You are an English person, John/Jane, visiting your penfriend Carlos/Carmen. You don't speak any Spanish. Your penfriend introduces you to another friend who looks very nice but doesn't speak any English. You would like to know something about him/her. Think of what questions you would like to ask.

B You are Carlos/Carmen and your penfriend, John/Jane, is visiting you. He/she doesn't speak any Spanish but you speak Spanish and English. You introduce John/Jane to another Spanish friend, Pedro/Patricia, who doesn't speak any English. How do you introduce them? If they want to communicate with each other you will have to act as interpreter.

C You are Pedro/Patricia and you don't speak any English. Your friend Carlos/Carmen introduces you to his/her English penfriend who looks very nice but doesn't speak any Spanish. You would like to know something about him/her. Think of what questions you would like to ask.

Situation two

A You are an English person on holiday in a foreign country. You don't feel well so you go to the doctor. You don't speak his/her language and the doctor doesn't speak English.

B You are a doctor. You don't speak English and now an English person has come to see you. Maybe another patient can help.

C You are a patient waiting to see the doctor. You can speak English.

(This idea is from *Mixed Ability Classes*, Luke Prodromou, Phoenix, 1992.)

Think of another situation for a bilingual ROLEPLAY with three characters.

4 Drama

Putting on sketches or plays requires different responses from different students. There are small and big parts to play, speaking parts and non-speaking parts. There may be a need for script writers, an artist, a props maker, a stage director, a costume designer, a prompt and so on depending on the type and scale of the performance.

On a smaller scale, students can be asked to act out a scene based on a picture or a short extract of dialogue.

Pictures

Students work in groups (mixed levels). You provide them with a picture in which there are at least two people. You can either give all the groups the same picture or different pictures. Give them a list of questions to discuss, e.g.

Where are these people?
What is their relationship?
What has just happened?
What is happening now?
What is going to happen?

The students discuss the questions in detail. You then ask them to act out a short scene between the people. This can provide for a little or a lot of dialogue between any number of people, depending on the students' interpretation of the picture. While all the students have been involved in creating the scene, not all need be involved in acting it out.

If each group used the same picture, they can compare interpretations after watching the different sketches and decide which one was best or most original. If they used different pictures, make sure they don't show the other groups their picture. Then display all the pictures and get the students to decide which scene matches which picture as the students act out their scenes.

Extracts of dialogue

This activity is similar, except the starting point for the scene they act out is a short dialogue. This should be very simple in terms of language but 'ambiguous' in terms of the topic. That is, it should not be obvious what the people are talking about, who they are or where they are from the dialogue. The students again discuss questions about the dialogue and then have to extend the dialogue, incorporating at some point the part they have read and then act it out.

Here are two examples of the type of dialogue you can use:

Example 1:
A: *Shh.*
B: *What?*
A: *Shh.*
B: *Oh no.*
A: *Did you hear that?*
B: *What?*
A: *Shh.*
B: *Aagh!*

Example 2:
A: *I don't want it.*
B: *But it's yours.*
A: *I don't care.*
B: *Here you are.*
A: *No!*
B: *All right.*

5 Responding to text

Students can be asked to produce in groups a written or oral response (e.g. a poster or a short ROLEPLAY) to something they have read or listened to. There are many examples of this type of activity and basically any text can be used.

Here are two ideas.

1 Listen to a song with a 'story' or a 'message' and do comprehension work on the lyrics. Students then create and act out a scene based on the song.
2 Read a poem, write a similar one and illustrate it. The poems you choose should be simple and appealing to the age group you are teaching. Below is the beginning of an animal alphabet poem (based on the idea in Edward Lear's An Animal Alphabet in *The Rattle Bag*, eds. Heaney S. and Hughes T., Faber and Faber 1982).

> A The Angry Artistic Ant,
>   who lived alone in an old apartment, and painted pictures
>   of apples and aeroplanes.
>
> B The Beautiful Beetle,
>   who always wore big blue boots when it didn't rain,
>   and forgot to wear them when it did.
>
> C The Calm Crazy Cow,
>   who cried and ate chocolate cake and curry in front of the fire
>   when she caught a cold.

● Ask the students to illustrate a verse you give them to check comprehension. They could do this through mime, a short sketch or a labelled picture.

● Then, in groups, they write another verse for a different letter and present it to the class in any way they like (written with a picture to illustrate it, read aloud with mime, etc.).

(Further suitable examples of 'fun' texts can be found in *Creative Grammar Practice* by Herbert Puchta and Günter Gerngross, Addison-Wesley Longman, 1992)

T A S K

Choose one of the ideas from this chapter to try with your class. While the activity is in progress, focus on one group in particular and consider these questions:

What did each of the students do?

How was this decided?

Did all the students participate equally? Why or why not?

Was this group a good mix in terms of different strengths, weaknesses and talents?

Evaluate the success of the activity. What changes would you make if you did it again?

CHAPTER 9

Open-ended activities

These are activities which are designed to let students respond at their own level. Unlike graded tasks, they do not require production of different worksheets, although the principle of letting students work at their own level is the same. Students work individually, in pairs or in groups at their own level on the same task. Most, but not all, require the student to produce language.

1 Diaries or student journals

Students can keep a diary, journal or personal notebook in English. At low levels it is probably a good idea to set a topic for each entry, e.g. *My hobbies*, *My family*, *What I did at Christmas*, etc. although later on they could choose what to write about. The aim is to get the students to write whatever they can on the topic in a certain time. This can be done either in class time (e.g. ten minutes at the beginning or end of a lesson) or, when the students are used to it, at home.

The emphasis should be on FLUENCY rather than ACCURACY so any feedback you give (e.g. written comments) should focus on responding to content rather than form. You can of course make a note of common problems to deal with later on. By not correcting every error, you will hopefully encourage the students to become more confident in their ability to express themselves in writing.

Here are some extracts from some students' journals with the teacher's responses. The different levels of language ability are clear.

Older students can use the diary to reflect on their learning and progress.

2 Choosing vocabulary to learn

After dealing with general comprehension of a reading text, give the students bilingual dictionaries and set a time limit. They have to choose which words they want to look up and learn. Stronger students will work more quickly and get through more words. Make sure everybody has looked up a minimum of three words, then get students to teach their words to their partner.

3 Asking or answering questions

Question lists

These could be questions about anything and to practise any language. Give the students a long list. Within a time limit they have to answer as many as they can. The questions you want everyone to answer should be the first ones in the list, or, if the questions are in sections, ask the students to answer at least one from each section. The questions can become progressively more difficult. Here are some examples of questions in the present tense on personal information.

You and your family

What's your name? Have you got any brothers or sisters? If yes, what are their names? How old are they?

School

Do you like school? Why or why not? What are your favourite subjects? Which subjects don't you like?

Daily routines

What time do you get up? What do you have for breakfast?
What time do you get home? What do you do after school?
What do you usually eat in the evening?
What are your favourite TV programmes?
What time do you go to bed in the week?

Holidays

Where do you usually go on holiday in the summer?
Who do you go with? How long do you spend there?

Wall crawl

A wall crawl is a reading task where students have a list of questions to answer using information that is displayed on the wall. This can be a mixture of visual and written information. It is good for livening up a reading activity and to practise the skill of scanning (reading for specific information). Set a time limit then, for checking, put students together who have answered approximately the same number of questions.

Find someone who ...

This is a mingling activity in which students stand up and go round asking questions to find someone who answers *yes* to their question. For example, to practise the present perfect for experience contrasted with the past simple:

Find someone who ...	Name	When?/Where?/Who?
... has been to England		
... has ridden a horse		
... has broken a bone		

Everybody has to ask the question *Have you ever ...?* to complete the name column. Weaker students may then just ask *Who?* or *When?* and answer these questions with one word whereas stronger students should ask and answer in full.

4 Dictation and questions

- Dictate some words or phrases linked to a particular factual topic to the class one by one. As you dictate them, ask for volunteers to come up and write them on the board. Start with the most difficult ones as stronger students will volunteer first. No one is allowed to come up to the board more than once.
- You should end up with a board like this:

Washington DC	*in San Francisco*	*red, blue and white*
the Big Apple	*Bill Clinton*	*the White House*
		yellow
on the east coast	*dollars and cents*	*Hollywood*

- Once the words are on the board, the students have to try to guess the question you are thinking of to elicit each answer. (Write down the questions you want to elicit first.) Once you have got the correct questions, drill them and tell the students they must try to remember them without writing them down. As they practise each question, rub the answer off the board and display the question on an overhead projector (or gradually reveal a poster).
- Turn off the overhead projector (or take down the poster). Then ask for volunteers to repeat the questions in turn. Another student must volunteer the answer and come and write it on the board once again.
- When all the answers are written up again tell the students that they now have to write the questions. They can work individually or in same-level groups. Stronger students who finish this task quickly go on to write more questions about the USA or to write a short paragraph.

(Described by Shelagh Deller at the APPI conference in Porto, April 1996.)

5 Responding to a picture

Students have a picture and write around it words, expressions or phrases associated with it. This can be done to create interest in a reader or reading text, for example. To help them you can write in simple questions that they have to respond to. This can be done as an individual, pair or group activity.

6 Using stories

Stories appeal to all ages and abilities and can continue to hold fascination even when they have been listened to or read many times over. You can exploit this by using stories in English that the students already know in their own language. A variety of tasks can be used to allow students to respond at their own level.

- Students listen to the story in English, perhaps told with the help of pictures or mime. Then they have to draw a picture of the story and write either words, sentences or a paragraph next to the picture to summarise the main points.
- Students listen to the story then in groups have to act out a scene. This can be mimed or acted with dialogue or mimed with a narrator telling the story.
- You start to tell the story but after a while you ask a question and the students have to write their response while you pause. The questions asked allow weaker students to respond with perhaps a single word while stronger students may write a sentence or more. See PHOTOCOPIABLE PAGE 17 for an example.

There are various possible ways of following this.

- In mixed-level pairs or small groups students compare their responses to the questions, and produce a 'final version' for each one. Retell the story and elicits the response from each group. The whole class chooses the best one.

- Grouped according to their different levels, students write the story. Provide weaker students with a gapped text, middle-level ones with keywords while stronger ones write from scratch.
- In mixed-level groups the students write the story or act it out.

7 Using video

Video may be easier to understand than audio listening material because of the visual clues. It can therefore be very useful for mixed-ability classes, particularly building confidence in those students who find listening difficult.

Here are two tasks which allow open-ended responses.

- Show the students a short video scene or part of a scene, preferably one in which there is quite a lot happening or a story developing. As they watch they write down as many words, expressions or sentences as occur to them. Elicit their ideas onto the board, nominating the weaker students first to contribute. You should end up with a board full of language notes. In mixed groups the students write a summary of the story so far, then act out a continuation.
- Show the students a video sequence and give them some sentence beginnings which they have to complete. Again, this offers possibilities for very brief responses or more extended ones. In mixed level-groups the students compare and correct their responses.

8 Vocabulary brainstorming

This can be done from a picture or from a topic title. Within a time limit students (individually or in pairs) write down as many words as they can associated with the picture or topic. Elicit ideas onto the board, nominating first the weaker students to answer. Check that everyone understands the meaning of the words, the part of speech and knows how to say them.

9 Poetry writing

This procedure can be followed for a wide variety of topics. In terms of preparation you need to find a poem on a theme that you think will appeal to your students and that they will be able to understand quite easily. If you use authentic material such as the poem below there may be some language that is above their level: explain it in English or use L1. The appeal of this poem in fact is its simplicity, length, humour and the strong rhyme.

- Write the topic on the board, e.g. ducks.
- Now the students think individually about the topic and write down as many words or phrases associated with it as they can. If they don't know the words in English, they can write them in L1 or ask for help. If necessary, ask some questions to help them, e.g.

  What do ducks look like? Where do they live?
  What noise do they make? How do they move?
  Are they serious or funny? What stories do you know about ducks?

- Students now compare their ideas in pairs and add to their individual lists.
- Elicit from each pair two words or expressions and put them on the board so that the board is full of language. Feed in English words as necessary. You should have only English words written on the board. Read aloud the words and expressions as the students listen.
- Tell the students to make up a short poem about ducks using any of the language on the board or that in their original list. This can be done individually or in pairs. Monitor and help as necessary. Weaker students will be able to rely totally on the language already given on the board whereas stronger ones may still add their own ideas.

- Ask if anyone would like to read their poem out loud. It is probably best not to force anyone.

- Show them the poem you found and read it out loud to them. Ask them how it compares to their own poem. Do comprehension work as necessary.

The poem below contains some unusual language but can easily be explained or illustrated. A good task might be to get the students to order some pictures, like the ones below.

The Duck   (Ogden Nash)

Behold the duck.
It does not cluck.
A cluck it lacks.
It quacks.
It is specially fond
Of a puddle or a pond.
When it dines or sups,
It bottoms ups.

(From *The Rattle Bag*, eds. Heaney S. and Hughes T., Faber and Faber, 1982.)

10 Music

You can use music in the same way as a visual stimulus. AUDITORY LEARNERS may be more responsive to this in fact.

- Give the students a list of questions to think about as they listen to a piece of music. This should be instrumental, i.e. without lyrics. Tell them it is OK to write some things in L1 if they don't know how to say them in English.

  Close your eyes and listen to this piece of music. Answer these questions in as much detail as possible. Where are you? What can you smell around you? What can you hear? How do you feel? What can you see?
  Now listen again. Some people are in your scene. How many people are there? What do they look like? Who are they? What are they doing? How are they feeling? They are talking. What are they talking about?

- After they have listened enough times to answer the questions the students compare their ideas in groups. They can also help each other with how to say things in English. You can monitor and help too. Then ask the students to act out a scene to go with the music. This can be with or without dialogue.

11 Student presentations

Students can be asked to do a presentation to the class at some time during the year. This can take different forms:

... a talk, with or without accompanying visuals (slides, photos, etc.)
... a poster presentation
... a demonstration followed by questions from the audience.

Since the format and content is flexible students can respond at their own level. The topic should be chosen by the student but should be something related to him or herself, e.g. a hobby or a personal experience. If students are doing this for the first time, it may be better for them to work in small groups.

T A S K

Either: Look back at section 6. Think of a story that you could use with one of your classes and write it out in English. Include about ten questions for the students to answer. **Or:** Find a simple English poem that you could use with your class, following the procedure in section 9.

CHAPTER 10

Dealing with different learning speeds

One of the problems that mixed-ability classes present for the teacher is that the students do not work at the same speed. Some take longer to understand and learn a new language point, or to do a practice activity or task, than others. If you work at the speed of the faster learners, the slower ones get left behind; if, on the other hand, you slow down to the pace of the slower learners, the stronger ones get bored and demotivated. If you go for the middle ground, you may end up catering for nobody! It is important to find a balance and clear strategies for ensuring that stronger students are not held back or challenged insufficiently, and that weaker students have enough time to do the essential work. In other words, you have to try and cater simultaneously for different learning speeds in the class.

1 Course content

As with any class, it is essential to plan work ahead. To begin with, you should have an overview of the year's objectives and the work to be covered. This information should be evident from the syllabus or, if you have no clearly defined syllabus, you will need to agree objectives and content with colleagues who are teaching the same level(s).

This then needs to be broken down into termly and perhaps half-termly objectives and content to enable you to plan ahead in manageable chunks.

Identify your syllabus

Depending on how your syllabus is organised, you need to identify how you will meet the objectives through, e.g.

CORE LANGUAGE input, new structures and vocabulary
core topics and tasks
core skills work, e.g. subskills of the four skills to be covered
core extensive reading
core learning behaviours.

'Core' refers to what is essential to achieving the objectives, i.e. work that needs to be done by everybody. Bear in mind, too, the obligatory assessment procedures used; if there are written tests at the end of the term, you will need to spend some time preparing students for these, although they shouldn't influence you so much so that you end up only doing exam preparation.

If you look at your coursebook, you will no doubt find that it contains more than enough work for the hours you have available. You may also find that not all of the language input and tasks are essential because they do not relate to the core input you have identified. Next to each core item on your syllabus write down the coursebook reference. Thus you will have selected the essential objectives and material for the term or half term.

Identify remedial work necessary

The next step is to consider what is essential **previous** knowledge for these objectives to be met. If your students are complete beginners – or assumed to be – this is not a problem. If, however, they are going into their second or third year of English, you need to identify any language items or skills that are essential background to the new core objectives for this year. You also need to note any materials references; perhaps there are activities in your coursebook or workbook which are suitable for this remedial work, or you may have to go to other supplementary sources.

Identify extra work

Thirdly, you need to think about extra work that can complement the core syllabus. It is essential that optional areas for extra study do not eat into the next block of core course work. If stronger students are allowed to race ahead with core course content, the problem of mixed ability just gets worse from term to term. So make sure the stronger students learn 'extra' things, not future core coursework. Again, note references to materials from the coursebook, workbook, supplementary materials and readers.

Assess the students

By now you have a three-part work plan: remedial, core and extra work. You will need to find out if your students – and which ones – actually need to do the remedial work. You can find this out by a test, or a number of MINI CHECKTESTS at the beginning of the year, or by setting tasks in class or for homework, or by a combination of these. ◆ SEE CHAPTER 11

As a general principle, it is probably not a good idea to begin the year with a lot of revision (especially if you don't even know if all the students need it) because it can bore the stronger students and further demotivate weaker students who see it as more of the same!

Inform the students

Give the students a copy or a simplified version of the document you have produced. Give them the remedial work list before the core work list for this year. This can provide a basis for:

… self assessment and a first individual counselling session
… choosing work for the first self-access sessions
… choosing homework.

The core work list can be used on an ongoing basis throughout the block of work: students can tick off areas as they cover them, evaluate their progress and refer back to the list for ongoing revision purposes.

The list of extra work will be most useful for the stronger students but should be given to everybody to avoid students feeling labelled as weak. You should make it clear that once the students are confident that they have learned what is listed on the remedial and core work lists, they can do work on this for homework, or in self-access sessions.

Students will obviously need training in using these checklists. Explaining the rationale, allocating class time to learner training generally and individual counselling sessions will help students take on this responsibility. Initially you may need to intervene if you see that students are seriously over- or underestimating their abilities.

Opposite is an example of a low-level remedial work checklist which focuses on areas of language knowledge and particular tasks that the students need to be able to do in the four skills.

YOU SHOULD ALREADY BE ABLE TO DO THE FOLLOWING:

Speaking
count from 1 to 20
identify colours
name ten classroom objects
give some basic personal information about yourself
identify members of your family
say the letters of the alphabet

Listening
understand simple questions about yourself and your family
write words as they are spelt out to you
follow instructions to colour a simple picture

Reading
match simple sentences to a picture of a classroom
identify true and false sentences about colours in a picture of a classroom
read a simple description of a family and match it to a picture

Writing
complete a form in English giving personal information
write a few sentences about yourself and your family
spell numbers 1-20, colours, classroom objects, family members correctly

---

Depending on the age and level of your students, the core work checklists can be more or less detailed. Whatever the level, it is a good idea to have them written in English, although you will need to check that all students understand what the terms refer to. Here is an example of a simple core work checklist.

BY THE END OF THIS TERM	
YOU SHOULD KNOW:	**YOU SHOULD BE ABLE TO:**
Structures *to be* *have got* present simple	**Speaking/listening** ask and answer questions about a family describe a person identify people on a photograph of a family from listening to a description draw a picture of a person as you listen to a description ask and answer questions about your daily routine listen to someone talking about their daily routine and fill in a chart ask and say what time it is
Vocabulary classroom objects jobs illnesses physical descriptions of people family daily routines the time	**Reading/writing** read a description of a family and match it to a family tree read short descriptions of people and match them to pictures write short descriptions of people in a picture write a short paragraph about you and your family read a short description of someone's routine and identify their job write a description of your daily routine write a description of the daily routine of another person in your family

Here is another more detailed checklist designed to help students evaluate their progress and identify any areas they need to work on.

Level:

Term:

Here is a list of this term's work. At the end of the term, tick off the areas we have covered and make a comment about your progress. You can say 'good' or 'satisfactory' or 'needs more work'.

	We did it	Comment
Language areas/speaking		
Talk about health and illness:		
parts of the body vocabulary		
illnesses and injuries vocabulary		
have got		
Make suggestions (1):		
Why don't you ...? + infinitive		
Say where things are:		
prepositions: *on, in front of, next to,*		
beside, in, under, on		
Talk about sports:		
different sports		
sports equipment		
Talk about clothes:		
clothes vocabulary		
to be wearing		
Describe actions happening now:		
present continuous		
Make and respond to suggestions (2):		
Let's + infinitive		
That's a good idea.		
Talk about entertainment:		
entertainments vocabulary		
musicians and musical instruments		
Listening		
understand the main points of a		
conversation		
understand specific details of a		
conversation		
Reading		
predict the topic of a text from the title		
and picture		
understand the main points of a text		
reorder a jumbled text		
guess the meaning of new words		
Writing		
write up the results of a class survey		
about sport		
make a poster about a concert		
write a short article about a pop group		

	We did it	Comment

Pronunciation
recognise and say *wh-* questions with
   falling intonation
link words ending in a consonant to
   those followed by a word beginning
   with a vowel
recognise and say the sounds /ɪ/
   and /e/
recognise and say the sounds /ɪ/
   and /iː/		

Learning skills speak in English in front of the class speak in English in a small group use classroom language copy correctly from the board keep well organised notes use a bilingual dictionary to check the meaning of new English words		
General Write a comment here about: your level of English the progress you have made this term your behaviour in class		

This task is best done with other colleagues teaching the same level. Follow the procedure outlined above for designing the checklists for remedial, core and extra work for the next half term's work.

2 Whole-class stages of the lesson

Although we have seen that individual work, pair and groupwork are very useful in the mixed-ability class, there will be some points at which the class will be working together with the teacher at the front, e.g.

... a teacher-led presentation of a new language point

... checking an exercise

... creating interest and brainstorming ideas prior to a skills-work activity.

The main aim here is to involve the stronger students as much as possible and make sure they do not get bored and to give the weaker students enough time and opportunities to understand and not get left behind.

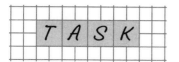

What do you do to make sure everyone is involved as much as possible in whole-class stages of the lesson? Compare your ideas with those below.

Presenting new language

- Elicit as much as you can from the stronger students to involve them and let them model the new language rather than doing it all the time yourself.

- Encourage peer correction.

- Insist on good pronunciation, particularly from the stronger students.

- Keep the presentation lively, fun and well-paced.
- Split the class if it becomes evident that the weaker students need a bit more oral practice; let the other students get on with a practice task individually or in pairs while you spend a little more time with part of the class.
- If it is evident that some students are not grasping the language, don't go on and on. Feeling embarrassed or stupid only creates further learning blocks. Move on to the practice activity where things may suddenly fall into place.

Checking an exercise

- It is not always productive to check through every classwork/homework exercise orally in class as this can slow the pace of your class and be a real waste of time for the students. Instead, they can check in mixed-level pairs or use a written key while you monitor to answer any specific questions or problems from students who had difficulties.
- If you do sometimes check through an exercise with the whole class:
  - … nominate weaker students to answer easier questions
  - … involve stronger students in explaining rather than doing it yourself
  - … don't let it go on too long: if some students have more questions, answer them later when the rest of the class is working on something else.

Creating interest and brainstorming ideas

- Allow thinking time: once you have established the theme and elicited a few ideas from the whole class, give the students time to think of more ideas individually or in pairs. Then elicit further ideas from the class, nominating the weaker students first.
- If stronger students say things which you think the weaker ones may not understand, get them to explain or paraphrase.

3 Fast finishers

Within any class and particularly a very mixed-level class it is inevitable that learners will take different amounts of time to complete the work set in class. Students who finish first may become restless or even disruptive if they are left doing nothing. This is also a waste of valuable learning time. It is therefore very important that you have a range of strategies to deal with fast finishers.

If you are using some of the options we have looked at such as graded tasks, self access, different responses or open-ended activities, then you should have fewer problems with fast finishers. However, when the whole class is doing the same activity (which at some point they will need to), there is likely to be a greater problem with students completing tasks at different times.

Also, bear in mind that it may not always be the stronger students who finish first.

Before reading on, think of how you deal with the problem of fast finishers in your classes. Make a list of different ideas. Then read on and compare.

Checking work

This is the first thing fast finishers should be encouraged to do.

- Fast finishers should be encouraged to check their own work. They may have error checklists to help them to do this. ◆ SEE PAGE 31

- Look at their work and tell them how many mistakes there are, without telling them what they are or where they are. They have to then try and find them.
- They can check their work with another student who has also finished. If the task is one in which there are right and wrong answers, and there are differences, they can try and work out who is right. If the task is a freer exercise they can look for any errors in each other's work.

Helping other students

You can ask fast finishers to go and help students who have not finished or who are finding the task difficult. This promotes co-operation between learners. It is important that right from the beginning you foster a sense of support and co-operation among learners rather than competition or resentment. ◆ SEE CHAPTER 2

Extension activities

It may be possible to extend some activities. Here are some ideas.

Reading comprehension

If students have been answering questions about a text, they could:

… write some more questions
… do another task which asks them to react to the text in some way, e.g. say if they liked the story and why
… draw a picture to go with it
… supply a different ending
… imagine the conversation between two people in the text
… say what they think happened next
… choose some words from the text to look up in their dictionaries
… write definitions for some of the words in the text and test other fast finishers.

Grammar exercises

If they have been doing an exercise to practise a specific structure, they could:

… write some more simple examples
… practise saying the sentences to another fast finisher (to practise pronunciation).

Writing

If they have written a paragraph about something, they could:

… write a little bit more
… write another one.

Vocabulary

If they have been doing some work on vocabulary on a particular topic, they could:

… think of more words associated with the topic in L1, then find out what they are in English (in a bilingual/picture dictionary)
… practise saying the words to another fast finisher to practise pronunciation
… do a specific pronunciation activity, e.g. group the words according to the number of syllables or where the stress is, or identify which words contain a particular sound.

Speaking

If they have been doing a pairwork speaking activity, they could:

… do it again (e.g. if it's a dialogue) in a different mood, sounding happy, angry, sad, bored, etc.
… write it down
… do it again, giving different answers to the questions (if it is a question and answer activity).

Listening comprehension

If they have been completing a task after a listening activity, they could:

... read through the tapescript

... write down any new words from the tapescript

... read the tapescript aloud in pairs.

Additional exercises

Most courses have more than enough work to get through in a year. Fast finishers can therefore do exercises that you have not had time to do with the whole class, especially those exercises from the part of the book you have already covered and know you won't want to use with the class. It is ideal if the book has a key so that students can check their own work. If it doesn't, they can check with another student. If they have any specific questions, they can ask you or make a note of them to ask later. It is important that you spend more time monitoring the work that the other students are still doing.

Some coursebooks nowadays have a special section of extra tasks for fast finishers and these are clearly ideal.

You can also of course make use of the extra work checklist (SEE PAGE 64) and ask students to select something from this to do.

Workcards/sheets

Have a collection of laminated workcards/sheets or photocopies of different exercises with you in your lessons. These could be taken from the self-access centre. Fast finishers can be given an activity, e.g. a crossword or other word puzzle to do while the other students are finishing off.

Readers

Fast finishers can get on with their reader. If you are doing one reader with the whole class, encourage stronger students to choose an additional reader from the self-access centre which they can read on their own at times like these.

4 Homework

Homework is important in any class but particularly so in mixed-ability classes. It is an ideal opportunity for slower students to catch up and an opportunity for stronger students who work quickly to do extra tasks.

The usual homework procedure used by teachers is to set the same task for everyone. In fact, the idea of the whole class doing the same homework is based on the assumption of a LOCKSTEP system of teaching or assessment (which assumes that everyone is learning the same things at the same rate). It is also easier for the teacher, in terms of selecting tasks to set and in terms of marking or giving feedback.

However, from the point of view of making the most of homework with a mixed-ability class, certain problems arise. It may:

... be too difficult for some students and too easy for others

... take some students a long time to do and others no time at all

... not be the most useful thing for everybody.

TASK Cover the ideas on page 71. How can you or do you solve these problems? Compare your ideas with those below.

Tie homework in with core work and plan ahead

- Homework tasks that everybody has to do should tie in with the core work you have outlined for the term.

- Try to ensure that homework tasks are fair, i.e. don't set tasks that you know all but the strongest students will do badly. You need to make sure you have done some learner training activities for homework tasks so that all learners are aware of suitable strategies to use. ◈ SEE CHAPTER 4 This means that it is important to plan what you will set for homework ahead of time.

- If some homework tasks are tied in with CONTINUOUS ASSESSMENT, it might be a good idea to set these tasks ahead of time and allow the students to complete them when they – and you – think they are ready to do so. This can be discussed in individual counselling sessions. ◈ SEE CHAPTER 11

Have some homework tasks that students can work on together

You can encourage students to work on some homework tasks together: there is no reason why homework should always be done individually.

Set time limits

You should set a minimum amount of time per week that should be spent on English homework. This could be agreed in a class contract at the beginning of the year. ◈ SEE PAGE 18 Students should be encouraged to keep a section of their notebook as a homework record in which they note down how much time they have spent on their homework and what they did.

You will need to look at the students' homework records. Students who are completing tasks quickly and well need to be encouraged to do more. You can use your 'extra work' checklist to direct students to additional tasks.

Sometimes students may be doing the work quickly but not very well: in that case you need to advise them on how to check their work carefully.

Students who are spending too long on the homework need to be made aware of this too. Try to find out why they are taking so long; it could be that they do not have a quiet place to work at home, for example.

Give the students a choice sometimes

In the same way that it is a good idea to allocate some class time to individual needs via self-access sessions, it is a good idea to allocate some homework time to this, too. Everyone should be told to refer to their lesson summary sheets and to the core work checklists to ensure they are up to date with what they are supposed to know. Stronger students can then choose to do work from their extra work checklists while weaker students can spend it on remedial work or revision of core work. Make sure they keep records of what they have done.

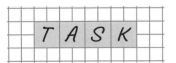

Look back at this chapter and select the three most important things that will help you deal with your mixed-ability class. If you can, compare and discuss your choice with a colleague.

CHAPTER 11

Assessment

Many teachers are worried about the question of assessment, particularly when it comes to mixed-ability classes. We will look at when and how students can be assessed.

1 Assessing at the beginning of the year

You may or may not be given information about students coming into your class. If not, you will certainly want to find out something about their language level to see whether you are dealing with a very mixed-level class or not. If you have been given assessment records, for example, it is probably still a good idea to gather some information yourself to complement this.

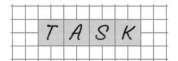

Cover the list below. What information do you usually want about the students' language level? How do you obtain this?

You may want information about:

... their knowledge of grammar
... their knowledge of vocabulary
... their ability in listening
... their ability in reading
... their ability in writing
... their ability in speaking.

In general terms you need to know if they are at the right level to begin the new year's work.

In addition you will want information about:

... their behaviour in class
... their motivation
... their learning style
... their awareness of effective learning strategies
... their interests and strengths in other areas.

We have seen ideas for gathering information about these things throughout the book. ◆ SEE PHOTOCOPIABLE PAGES 1, 4, 5, 7, 8, 9, 15

You can find out about their language level in the following ways.

Give them a formal test

Make up a test yourself or (preferably) with the help of colleagues. Alternatively, you may be able to use a published test, perhaps one from the end of the previous year's coursebook.

You may want to include sections on grammar and vocabulary, a reading comprehension, a listening comprehension and a writing task. A formal speaking test is more difficult to administer with a large class, although this could be done in small groups while the rest of the students are working on their own. You could ask the students being tested to carry out a short ROLEPLAY or a task in which they have to find out information from the other students by asking questions.

The test content should aim to assess whether students are at the required level for the beginning of this year. That is, it should test those language items and skills that you identified as things the students should already be able to do before beginning on the new year's work. ◆ SEE PAGE 63

Give them a series of MINI CHECKTESTS corresponding to their remedial work list. ◆ SEE PAGE 76

You could give students some choice over these. Give them the remedial work checklist first and get them to identify the two areas they are most confident about and the two they are least confident about. Then get them to do the corresponding MINI CHECKTESTS. It will be evident if they have seriously over- or underestimated their abilities from the results they get.

Test them informally through different classroom activities

Observe and keep a note of how students perform in different activities that you use. You will need to monitor their work carefully. Pay attention to any students you think may be particularly weak or strong to check your impression. This will take longer than giving a formal test but may give you a fairer picture of each student in the end.

A combination of the two approaches above is probably best.

If you discover that some students are extremely weak, and really not up to the level in any area, perhaps because they suffer from particular learning disadvantages such as hearing or sight problems or come from very disadvantaged backgrounds, then you need to see whether it is possible to put them in a special class for tuition or organise extra classes for them.

If these solutions are not possible, you will have to try to at least give them extra remedial work to do. You will need to give them guidance (via checklists and individual counselling) about what exactly they need to do. You should be able to provide them with materials and resources from the self-access collection for this.

If you find that some students are very strong (for example, bilingual children), then it is also worth exploring the possibility of different classes so that they are not held back. If this is not feasible or allowed within your school system, you will need to provide extra work for these students to challenge them appropriately. Students like this should be regarded as an asset to the class, not as a threat to you. Take advantage of their knowledge! Again, the use of checklists with extra study areas and tasks listed, individual counselling and library or self-access resources will be useful.

Individual counselling

As soon as possible in the year, you should try to have an individual counselling session with all the students. This offers opportunities for:

... getting to know the students
... showing them you are aware of them as individuals and concerned about their progress
... involving them in self evaluation and assessment
... motivating them
... advising them
... checking their work, homework records, etc.
... answering individual questions.

Explaining assessment procedures

You also need to introduce students to the assessment criteria that will be used during the year, e.g.

... how often will formal tests take place?
... what form will continuous assessment take?
... what criteria will you use in assessing students' work?

You may need to explain some of this in L1, particularly when explaining the rationale behind the assessment procedures. You should show them examples of criteria used in the assessment of different kinds of work, e.g. written work, oral work or groupwork (behaviour, etc.).

Here is an example.

GROUPWORK			
	Usually	Sometimes	Rarely
Uses English as much as possible			
Takes an active role in discussion			
Listens to others			
Gets on well with other group members			
Carries out tasks as allocated by group			
Overall comment:			

You may need to introduce the students to the idea of self evaluation and assessment if they have not done this before. Again, you can show them what they will use for this, e.g. self-access record sheets (PHOTOCOPIABLE PAGE 13), PROJECT WORK (PHOTOCOPIABLE PAGE 16), end-of-lesson summaries and checklists.

2 Testing throughout the year

You need to keep track of students' progress and achievement throughout the year. This is probably best done through a mixture of formal testing and CONTINUOUS ASSESSMENT. The following points are of particular relevance to mixed-ability classes.

Record-keeping

- It is essential that both you and the students keep a record of work they have covered. For example, if you have used graded tasks, you should know which level of difficulty was done each time. It was suggested before that colour coding is the best way of doing this. Similarly, with self-access activities, records should be kept of what students have done.

Counselling

- Individual counselling should be carried out. Students can contribute to this if they have been asked to keep records of work and evaluate their own performance as a matter of course (e.g. at the end of lessons, blocks of work, after self-access activities). Counselling can take place during self-access sessions or outside class time.

  SEE CHAPTER 13, APPRAISALS AND PERFORMANCE REVIEWS, IN *EVALUATING YOUR STUDENTS*, FROM THE SAME SERIES.

Checking progress

Students (and you) need to know where they are in terms of:

- their own progress. Have they improved since the beginning of the year?

- the standard expected of a class at this level. Are they weak, average or very strong for the level? It does not matter where they are in relation to the other students in the class and you should not focus on this since it can discourage those 'at the bottom' and make those 'at the top' complacent.

- Students need to know in which areas they are weak and need to improve (language, skills, behaviours). They should be given help and guidance on how to do this. If this is written down as a follow-up to an individual counselling session it can be referred back to and you and the student can see if the suggested action was taken and, if so, if it was successful.

Assessment records

Assessment records should be as complete as possible with references to different language skills, effort, progress and levels of achievement, e.g.

Student record	
Name Diego Garcia	Date 19·12·96

	Comment on effort, progress and achievement
Grammar	Some difficulties with accuracy work.
Vocabulary	Good. Wide range.
Listening	Very good.
Speaking	Fluency good — still needs to work on pronunciation.
Reading	Good.
Writing	Tends to be careless. Has made an effort to check work before handing in. Needs to work on this.
Participation/ behaviour	Co-operative and willing to contribute.
Learning skills	Needs to discipline himself to check work, use dictionary more.
Test results/ continuous assessment	Disappointing on grammar checktests and writing. Good on listening/speaking.
Homework	Careless at times, but generally does it.
General	Doing fine for the level. Needs to work on accuracy.

Formal tests

Formal tests can be designed to cater for mixed ability by:

- including progressively more difficult tasks so that the stronger students who work faster will be increasingly challenged.

- having within each section of the test an optional extra task so that students who have completed the 'core' test can go on to choose which extra parts to do, depending on the extra study areas they have completed on their learning checklist.

- having one extra task at the end.
- designing different tests for different levels within the class.

This final option is perhaps the least satisfactory since it involves considerably more work for the teacher.

Mini checktests

- MINI CHECKTESTS are very useful with a mixed-ability class. These are short tests which focus on discrete language items or particular tasks from the syllabus, e.g. one might test the students' ability to form questions in the present simple, another test a particular lexical set through a read-and-draw activity. You can write your own MINI CHECKTESTS or use exercises from grammar books or the students' workbook. They can be stored with the self-access materials and students can choose which ones to do. These should be colour-coded according to level of difficulty, and should also relate to core or extra study sections of the checklists provided. Use the same colour coding system as for graded tasks and self-access materials. Students can choose when they want to do one and they can also be redone at a later stage for remedial or revision purposes. You will need to provide answer keys.

Continuous assessment

CONTINUOUS ASSESSMENT can be used in conjunction with formal tests. This means that coursework throughout the year counts as much as results in a special end-of-term or end-of-year test.

One form of CONTINUOUS ASSESSMENT that works well with mixed-ability classes is this:

- Define at the beginning of the term a number of tasks related to core work that students will need to carry out successfully.
- Give students a list of these and give them a final date by which they must do them, but tell them that they can do them before if they feel ready.
- Let them have another go at the task if they do not complete it satisfactorily the first time. In this way it becomes a learning as well as testing tool.

3 Testing at the end of the year

In most school systems there is one test that all students in a class must do in order to pass satisfactorily to the next level. This makes no concessions to mixed-ability classes. Those students who have not reached the required standard as reflected in the test will inevitably do worse. However, this may not be as demotivating as it can be if the student:

… knows where he/she stands already in terms of level, through self evaluation, CONTINUOUS ASSESSMENT and counselling,

… has had recognition for effort and progress over the year in the teacher's assessment.

T A S K

What assessment procedures are currently used with your mixed-ability class(es)? Which ideas from this chapter would be the most useful ones to include in your system?

Solving the problems

In the introduction to this book, we described the term 'mixed ability' as referring to a variety of types of differences among our learners. Then we saw that there is not one easy answer to the question *How should I deal with my mixed-ability group?* This is what has been covered in this book.

On pages 5 and 6, we looked at problems created by mixed-ability classes. We will see now if we can suggest solutions to those problems.

TASK | Before reading on, look back at the problems that you identified as important for you. Can you now suggest two or three solutions to those problems? Write them down then compare them with the suggestions that follow.

Half the students have finished an exercise when the other half have only just begun.

The use of graded tasks here would help (CHAPTER 5). If stronger students are given more challenging work to do, it is less likely that they will finish quickly. Open-ended activities (CHAPTER 9) also allow students to respond at their own level and should keep stronger students occupied. Fast finishers should be set extra tasks, never just left doing nothing (CHAPTER 10).

The stronger students get bored if I spend time explaining to the weaker ones.

You can get the stronger students involved by getting **them** to explain: making sure that all students are involved is part of good classroom management (CHAPTER 1). You also need to pace whole-class teacher-led stages carefully (CHAPTER 10). Or have the students doing different things in the class: while you spend time 'teaching' a group of weaker students, the stronger students can be doing another task from the self-access centre (CHAPTER 6).

We've got a syllabus to get through but most of the students are already behind.

Planning your core coursework is essential (CHAPTER 10) and it is important that you do not begin every year with remedial work that not everybody needs. You do, however, need to cater for those students who are behind by drawing up remedial checklists (CHAPTER 10), identifying gaps in the students' knowledge (CHAPTER 11) and providing opportunities for them to work on these areas in, e.g. extra classes, self-access slots and homework tasks.

The stronger students dominate.

Once again, ensuring that all students have the opportunity to participate is part of good classroom management (CHAPTER 1). Ensure that weaker learners have the opportunity to contribute in whole-class stages by asking them easier questions. Individual work, group and pairwork may be less threatening for quieter or weaker students. The use of graded tasks (CHAPTER 5), self-access (CHAPTER 6), content teaching (CHAPTER 7), different responses (CHAPTER 8) and open-ended activities (CHAPTER 9) encourage and provide opportunities for all students to contribute.

The weaker students sit at the back and start disrupting the lesson.

Good classroom management skills, the use of different groupings and interaction patterns (CHAPTER 1) and good lesson planning in terms of appropriate and varied task design should prevent this (CHAPTER 3 AND ALL OF PART B).

The weaker students don't even try.

Motivation is crucial (CHAPTER 2). Providing tasks which are achievable encourages students to try (GRADED TASKS, CHAPTER 5 AND OPEN-ENDED ACTIVITIES, CHAPTER 9). Recognising effort and progress is also an important factor (LEARNER TRAINING, CHAPTER 4, SELF-ACCESS, CHAPTER 6 AND ASSESSMENT CHAPTER 11).

I don't know where to pitch my lesson.

If you are working to a syllabus, then basically you have to deal with the language and skills that appear on it. You can adapt particular tasks to suit different levels of ability (GRADED TASKS, CHAPTER 5 AND OPEN-ENDED ACTIVITIES CHAPTER 9). Self access (CHAPTER 6) also allows students to work on different tasks at an appropriate level. In LOCKSTEP stages of the lesson make sure that you cater for all levels (SEE CHAPTER 10) by making sure everyone is involved.

The weaker students are always asking me things in their own language and want everything explained in it.

You need to vary your approach to cater for different learning styles (CHAPTER 3). By doing this you may discourage students from needing to have things explained. Insist that the students use English as much as possible. Raising their awareness of good learning strategies helps (CHAPTER 4) and also their awareness of the assessment criteria (CHAPTER 11). You also need to ensure your language is well graded (SEE CLASSROOM MANAGEMENT, CHAPTER 1).

Some of the weaker students try so hard but they still get bad marks.

Recognition of effort and progress is as important as achievement. This must be included in any evaluation of them (CHAPTER 11).

When I'm doing pair or groupwork I don't know whether it's better to put strong and weak students together or put students of the same level in the groups.

There is no one right answer to this. It depends on the activity and the stage of the activity (SEE ALL OF PART B).

Some of the students' written homework is an absolute disaster – grammar, spelling, everything! I don't know where to start correcting it.

If weaker students have been given no guidance, this is not surprising. Train students in error awareness and encourage them to check and correct their own and each other's work, using error checklists and reference books (CHAPTER 4). They need to be aware of the assessment criteria you use (CHAPTER 11). With freer, open-ended writing tasks, responding to the content and reformulation is more appropriate than correcting errors overtly.

Some of the really good students sometimes ask me difficult questions and one even corrected me once!

Good students should be regarded as a positive influence, not a threat. Get them on your side and give them credit for being good. If you don't know the answer to a question, don't be afraid to say so, but promise to find out. If you have reference books available in the class (which is often a good idea), then get the students to look the answer up.

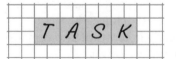

T A S K

Look back through the book and choose three ideas that you would like to implement. Decide when and how you will do this.

If you have colleagues who have also read this book, hold a meeting to exchange ideas on what you have read and to identify ideas that you would all like to try out. Then decide who will do what.

Good luck!

1 Learning English

SEE PAGE 8

Complete the questionnaire. Compare your answers with a partner.
Explain your answers.

	Yes	Maybe	No
I want to learn English.			
I enjoyed my English classes last year.			
I am a good student of English.			
I sometimes use English out of school.			
I think English is easy.			
I like trying to speak English.			
I liked my English teacher last year.			
I think English is useful.			
I expect to do well in my English class this year.			
I think learning English can be fun.			

2 English and your language

SEE PAGE 16

How do you say these things in your language? How do you say them in English?
Use the word box to help you.

taxi pizza hotel café hamburger football TV video radio
stop telephone Coca-Cola CD chocolate rock music

The Mixed Ability Class, © Julie Tice, 1997

3 Class survey

SEE PAGE 19

Find out how many of us have sisters.

✂

Find out how many of us have brothers.

Find out how many of us have pets.

Find out how many of us have computers.

Find out how many of us have bicycles.

Find out how many of us can swim.

Find out how many of us can ride a horse.

Find out how many of us can dive.

Find out how many of us can rollerskate.

Find out how many of us can play a musical instrument.

Find out how many of us like hamburgers.

Find out how many of us like vegetables.

Find out how many of us like fish.

Find out how many of us like milk.

Find out how many of us like coffee.

Find out how many of us walk to school.

Find out how many of us go to bed after eleven o'clock.

Find out how many of us watch TV every day.

Find out how many of us get up before seven o'clock.

Find out how many of us talk in our sleep.

Find out how many of us have been to a foreign country.

Find out how many of us have broken a bone.

Find out how many of us have won a competition.

Find out how many of us have been to a pop concert.

Find out how many of us have seen a famous person.

4 How we like to learn English

Write *yes*, *no* or *sometimes* under each picture.

in groups

listening to cassettes

seeing new words

doing tests

reading books

practising pronunciation

doing and making things

alone

hearing new words

doing projects

acting

writing

doing grammar exercises
in the book

speaking in pairs
or groups

listening to the
teacher

watching videos and
answering questions

Now write and draw three more things: one you always like doing, one you sometimes like doing and one you **don't** like doing.

yes

sometimes

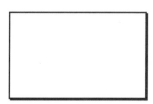
no

The Mixed Ability Class, © Julie Tice, 1997

Comments on the lesson

What we learned or practised today:

....

....

....

The activities we did:

1 ....   4 ....

2 ....   5 ....

3 ....

What I liked best was:

....

....

because ....

....

I didn't like: ....

because ....

....

I would like to do more:

....

....

....

6 Recording and remembering vocabulary

SEE PAGE 29

Here are some different ways of making vocabulary notes.

Place	What you do
cinema	see a film
chemist's	buy medicine
bank	get money
disco	go dancing
theatre	see a play
garage	buy petrol

Word	LI	Sentence
hot (adj.)	....	It's very *hot* in summer.
sunny (adj.)	....	It's *sunny* today.
cloud (n)	....	*Clouds* are white or grey.
snow (v)	....	It *snows* in the winter.
rain (v)	....	It *rains* a lot in the north.

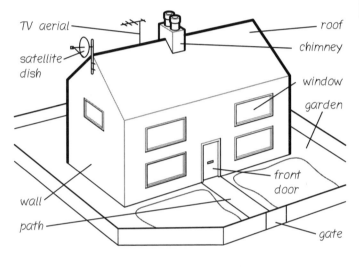

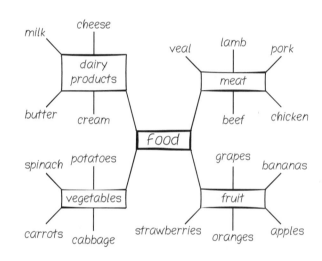

Word	Opposite
expensive	cheap
beautiful	ugly
thick	thin
funny	serious
strong	weak

Word	Picture	Sentence
long hair		She's got long hair.
curly hair		She's got curly hair.
a beard		He's got a beard.
bald		He's bald.

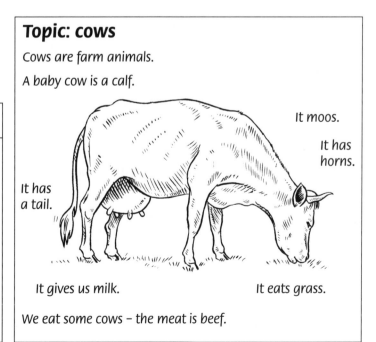

Topic: cows

Cows are farm animals.

A baby cow is a calf.

It moos.

It has horns.

It has a tail.

It gives us milk.

It eats grass.

We eat some cows – the meat is beef.

The Mixed Ability Class, © Julie Tice, 1997

7 Listening: What do you do?

SEE PAGE 32

You are talking in English to a very nice girl/boy you meet on holiday.

1 He/she is speaking very quickly. What do you do?
a) Look at the floor. ☐
b) Ask him/her to speak more slowly. ☐
c) Nod and pretend to understand. ☐

2 He/she uses a word you don't understand. Do you:
a) ignore it? ☐
b) ask what it means immediately? ☐
c) wait and see if it seems to be important or not? ☐

3 He/she uses lots of words you don't understand.
What do you do?
a) Ask him/her to speak more simply because your
English isn't very good. ☐
b) Say nothing. ☐
c) Get out your dictionary. ☐

4 You want to ask about something but you're not sure what the
word is in English. Do you:
a) decide not to ask? ☐
b) say you don't know the word in English and say the
word in your own language? ☐
c) try to describe it? ☐

5 Your friend is looking at you strangely after you said something.
Do you:
a) look strangely at him/her? ☐
b) say 'Did you understand what I said?' ☐
c) stay quiet. ☐

Read how two students write a composition. Who is the better student? Why?

Anna

She leaves her composition until the day before she has to give it to the teacher.	She sits down in front of the TV. It's her favourite programme.	She looks at the title of the composition.	She writes two sentences.

She watches TV.	She writes a few more sentences. She thinks there are some mistakes in the grammar. Never mind, the teacher will correct it if it's wrong.	She's not sure how to spell this, never mind. One more sentence.	OK, finished. She puts it in her bag and watches TV.

Sofia

The weekend before she has to give it to the teacher, she sits on her own in the kitchen. She looks at the title. She thinks a bit.	Then she writes a few ideas onto a piece of paper, in no particular order. She looks up a couple of words in the dictionary and writes those down.	Then she has a sandwich and goes to watch TV.	The next day she looks at what she wrote. She adds some more ideas. Then she decides how to order her ideas. She starts to write.

There are some words she's not sure about so she looks them up in her dictionary.	When she has finished writing, she reads carefully through her composition. She crosses some things out and changes one or two sentences.	Then she looks back at her notes from other written work. She makes sure she hasn't made any of the same mistakes.	Finally, she writes out her composition onto a clean piece of paper and puts it in her bag.

What do you do? Discuss it with your partner.
Who has got the best writing habits?

9 Work summary

SEE PAGE 33

Summary of my work

Name: Level:

Dates from: to:

	How good am I at this now?
Language areas we have covered: vocabulary	....
	....	....
grammar	....
	....	....
Skills work we have done: speaking	....
	....	....
listening	....
	....	....
reading	....
	....	....
writing	....
	....	....
Learning skills we have practised: using a dictionary	....
using error checklists	....
using classroom language	....
using the self-access materials	....
other	....

How have I behaved in class?

....

Have I completed all the homework?

....

What do I need to do to improve?

....

86

The Mixed Ability Class, © Julie Tice, 1997 **PHOTOCOPIABLE**

Multiple-choice text

Friday 13th November
15th
30th

What a day! My alarm clock didn't ring so I overslept. I got up at
sound / wake up
hear / woke up

nine o'clock / with a terrible headache. I suddenly remembered I had an
ten o'clock / backache.
twelve o'clock / toothache.

appointment with the dentist   at   quarter past twelve. I ran out of
doctor   quarter past ten.
hairdresser   quarter to ten.

the house and down the road.   Then I saw some people   laughing at me.
street.   children
path.   girls

I looked up.   I was still in my pyjama trousers. I was very confused.
round.   red.
down.   embarrassed.

I ran back home but then I found I didn't have my keys. I couldn't
knew
saw

open the door.   I got a ladder from the garden   and started to
window.   neighbour
gate.   garage

climb up to my bathroom   window. But the ladder was very new and it broke.
bedroom   nice
sitting room   old

I fell off and broke my leg.   Now I'm in hospital. My head   still
fall off   neck.   back
fell down   arm.   tooth

hurts and my leg   hurts too.
neck
arm

Gapped text

...............November

What a .... My .... I woke up

didn't ring so I ....

at .... with a terrible ....

I suddenly .... an appointment ....

.... at .... ten. I ran

.... and down .... laughing at me.

Then I .... laughing at me.

I .... I was .... my .... I ran

.... I was very .... but then I ....

have my keys. I couldn't .... I got a

.... from the .... and started ....

.... my bedroom .... But the

.... was very old and I

.... and broke .... Now I'm

.... My tooth .... and my

.... too.

Graded picture dictation

SEE PAGE 36

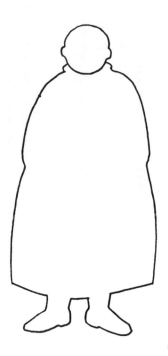

The Mixed Ability Class, © Julie Tice, 1997

12 Watching a video

SEE PAGE 41

Write about the video you are watching.

1 Name of programme:

....

2 Type of programme (cartoon, news, comedy, etc.):

....

3 Did you enjoy watching the programme?
very much ☐   quite ☐   not really ☐

4 Was the programme easy to understand?
very ☐   quite ☐   not very ☐

5 Was the programme
funny? ☐   serious? ☐
frightening? ☐   interesting? ☐
Other ....

6 What was the programme about?

....
....
....
....

7 What was the most interesting part of the programme?

....
....
....
....

8 Watch the programme again and note down any new words and expressions that you hear.

9 Talk about these with a partner or ask the teacher to help you understand them.

13 Self-access record

SEE PAGE 43

Date	What I plan to do in self access	Why	What I did in self access (and time spent)	Student comment	Teacher comment

The Mixed Ability Class, © Julie Tice, 1997

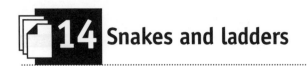

14 Snakes and ladders

SEE PAGE 48

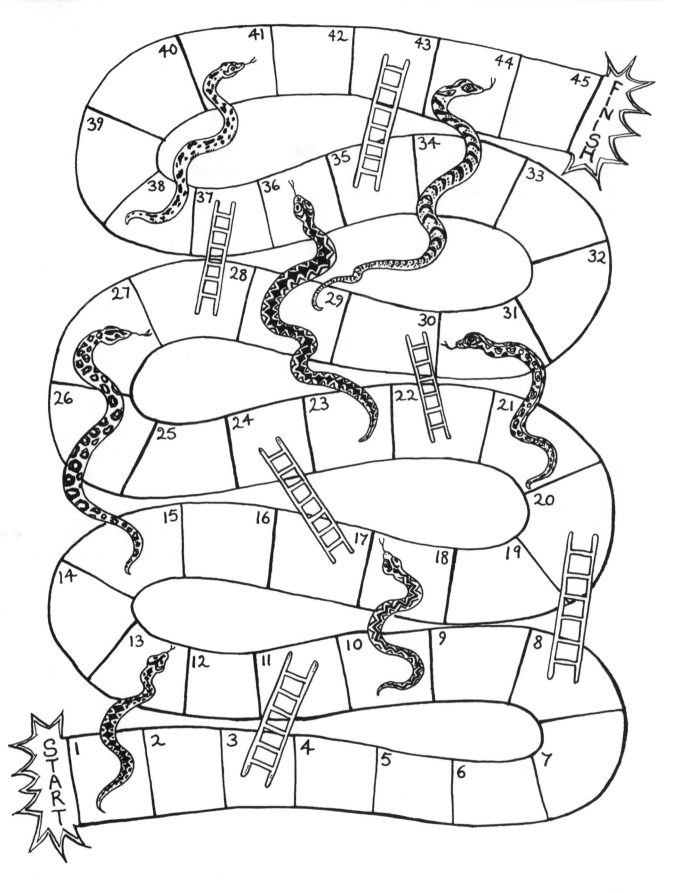

15 Students' interests

Write a number (1–4) next to each of the following topics.

1 = you are very interested in it.
2 = you are quite interested.

3 = you are not very interested.
4 = you are not at all interested.

 fashion ☐

 pop music ☐

 football ☐

 pets ☐

 history ☐

 famous people ☐

 the environment ☐

 wild animals ☐

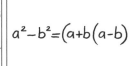 mathematics ☐

 kings and queens ☐

 how people live in different countries ☐

 cookery ☐

 science ☐

 inventions ☐

 geography ☐

 explorers and discoverers ☐

 stars and planets ☐

 cities in the world ☐

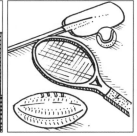 sport ☐

 technology ☐

Write down three more topics that you are interested in.

....

Planning project work

Group members: .... Project: ....

....

Planning

What we need to do	Who	Action/materials needed
1	....	....
2	....	....
3	....	....
4	....	....
5	....	....
6	....	....
7	....	....
8	....	....
9	....	....
10	....	....

Progress

What we have done	Comment
1	....
2	....
3	....
4	....
5	....
6	....
7	....
8	....
9	....
10	....

Evaluation

Did the group work well together?............................. What was difficult?.............................

Did I take an active part? .... What did I learn fom this project?.............................

Did I use as much English as possible? .... What do I need to do to improve?

What did I find easy?............................. ....

Comment on the final project: ....

....

The Mixed Ability Class, © Julie Tice, 1997 **PHOTOCOPIABLE**

Little Red Riding Hood

Once upon a time there was a girl called Little Red Riding Hood.

(What was Little Red Riding Hood like?)

One day her mother said to her: 'Little Red Riding Hood, I want you to go and visit your grandmother. She's not very well so I'd like you to take her a basket of food.'
'Yes, of course, mummy,' said Little Red Riding Hood. So her
mother prepared a basket of food.   **(What did she put in it?)**

Later that morning Little Red Riding Hood set off with her basket.
As she was walking through the forest singing she met the woodcutter,
then she met a stranger.   **(What did he look like?)**

'Good morning, sir,' she said brightly.
'Good morning, little girl,' he said. 'And where are you going?'   **(What did she reply?)**

'I see,' he said.
'Good day, sir. I must hurry now.' And she set off walking.
The stranger ran off very fast, which she thought was odd.
Some time later she arrived at her grandmother's house.   **(Describe the house.)**

'That's funny,' she thought. 'Why is the door open?' She pushed it gently
and saw her grandmother lying in bed, so in she went.
'Hello, grandmother. I've brought you some nice food.'
'Thank you, dear,' replied the grandmother in a funny voice.
Little Red Riding Hood looked at her grandmother. She looked funny.
'Grandmother, what big eyes you've got.'
'All the better to see you with, my dear.'
'And what big ears you've got.'   **(What did her grandmother reply?)**

'And, my goodness, what big teeth you've got.'
'All the better to eat you with.' And grandmother jumped out of bed
and pulled off her nightcap and nightgown. It wasn't her grandmother
at all. It was a big ugly wolf.   **(What did Little Red Riding Hood shout?)**

At that moment the door burst open and in ran the woodcutter with his axe.
When the wolf saw him, he was frightened and ran away.
    (What did the woodcutter say to Little Red Riding Hood?)

Then they heard a noise coming from the cupboard – it was grandmother's voice.
    (What did she say?)

They opened the cupboard. Grandmother was all right. So they all
hugged each other then they sat down and ate the food that was in
Little Red Riding Hood's basket.
It was the last time any of them ever saw the wolf, too. **(Why? What happened to the wolf?)**

And they all lived happily ever after.

Glossary

ACCURACY
If the teacher or the student or a learning activity is focusing on accuracy, it means that the main concern is on correctness of form and use. (see FLUENCY)

ANALYTICAL LEARNER
An analytical learner likes problem solving and working things out for him/herself.

AUDITORY LEARNER
One way of classifying different types of learner is by identifying which sense (visual, auditory, kinesthetic) they seem to respond to in terms of helping them learn and remember things. Auditory learners respond well to sound.

AUTHORITY-ORIENTED LEARNER
An authority-oriented learner sees the teacher as an authority figure. He/she likes clear structure and progression to a course.

BRAINSTORM
To think about a topic for a few minutes and collect as many ideas/words related to it as possible, without organising the ideas at all.

COMMUNICATIVE LEARNER
A communicative learner likes learning through group and social activities.

CONCRETE LEARNER
He/she learns best from visual and verbal experiences, and physical involvement.

CONTINUOUS ASSESSMENT
This means that examples of students' work are looked at throughout the term or year and grades given. Thus assessment of the student does not depend on their result in, e.g. one big end-of-year test. Continuous assessment should offer a more accurate reflection of a student's performance.

CORE LANGUAGE
Those items necessary for the student to be able to learn the syllabus and progress.

CUISENAIRE RODS
Small rods in a variety of colours and lengths, often used in teaching. Different length/colour rods can be used to represent language parts, e.g. syllables, endings.

ERROR AWARENESS
If you do not know that you are making mistakes in a foreign language, then you will not be able to correct them and therefore improve. Error awareness, or being able to recognise errors or mistakes in the language, is therefore very important for anyone who wants to make progress.

FLUENCY
If the focus is on fluency, it means that the emphasis is on 'getting the message across' or effective communication. Thus minor mistakes of, e.g. pronunciation or grammar are not important if they do not interfere with the message. (see ACCURACY)

KINESTHETIC LEARNER
(See also AUDITORY and VISUAL LEARNERS.) Kinesthetic learners are those who learn and remember best by doing, i.e. by actual experience.

LEARNING STRATEGIES
Techniques and procedures that learners use in order to help themselves learn.

LOCKSTEP
This refers to a type of teaching in which the whole class works at the same pace on the same task. The tasks and pace are set by the teacher and the teacher directs what is happening in the class.

MINI CHECKTEST
This is a small, short test, usually on a discrete language point, to assess students' comprehension of what has been taught.

PERSONALISATION
Using language to talk about yourself. New language is more meaningful and easier to remember if the student has related it to him/herself in this way.

PRESENTATION (1)
The stage of the lesson in which a new language point is introduced and explained to the students.

(2)
A student presentation means that the student stands up in front of the class to give a prepared talk or demonstration about a particular topic.

PROJECT WORK
A large task, composed of a number of smaller tasks and using a variety of skills, with some kind of end product such as the making of a video or a magazine.

ROLEPLAY	A spoken exercise (usually) where the students take on the roles of other people, e.g. a customer and a shopkeeper, in order to practise a language point in a more authentic fashion.
VISUAL LEARNER	Those who learn and remember best by seeing, i.e. reading the language.

Further reading

Britten, N *Who Knows?* Addison-Wesley Longman 1990
A book of quiz questions on a wide range of topics. Very motivating.

Campbell, C and Kryszewska, H *Learner-based Teaching* OUP 1992
Ideas for various activities which are based on information or material created by the learners themselves. Plenty of opportunities for personalisation, open-ended responses and groupwork.

Ellis, G and Sinclair, B *Learning to Learn English* CUP 1989
A very useful book on learner training. Geared towards adult learners but some of the ideas can be adapted for younger learners.

Gerngross, G and Puchta, H *Creative Grammar Practice* Addison-Wesley Longman 1992
Varied activities based on stimulating short texts for learning and practising grammar patterns.

Hadfield, J *Classroom Dynamics* OUP 1992
A resource book of ideas for creating a positive learning atmosphere and sense of group identity. Geared mainly towards adult multilingual classes but there are some ideas suitable for younger monolingual learners.

Haines, S *Projects* Addison-Wesley Longman 1989
A good practical guide to doing project work in your classes.

Harris, M and McCann, P *Assessment* Heinemann 1994
A useful book which looks at the key areas of formal and informal assessment and self-assessment.

Morgan, J and Rinvolucri, M *Once Upon a Time* CUP 1983
Different ideas for using stories with your students.

Murphey, T *Music and Song* OUP 1992
Varied and motivating ideas for using music and songs.

Prodromou, L *Mixed Ability Classes* Phoenix 1992
Lots of practical teaching ideas.

Sheerin, S *Self-access* OUP 1989
A useful guide to setting up a self-access centre and a collection of practical ideas for activities to include.

Willing, K *Teaching How to Learn* NCELTR 1989
A very useful book on learner training. Geared towards adult immigrants in Australia but some of the ideas can be used or adapted for use with younger monolingual learners.

Index of activities and topics

(numbers in brackets refer to photocopiable pages/activities)